The World of
Picasso

TIME LIFE BOOKS ®

TIME-LIFE LIBRARY OF ART

The World of Picasso 1881-1973

by Lael Wertenbaker
and
the Editors of TIME-LIFE BOOKS

TIME-LIFE BOOKS, Alexandria, Virginia

Time-Life Books Inc.
is a wholly owned subsidiary of
TIME INCORPORATED

FOUNDER: Henry R. Luce 1898-1967

Editor-in-Chief: Henry Anatole Grunwald
Chairman of the Board: Andrew Heiskell
President: James R. Shepley
Editorial Director: Ralph Graves
Vice Chairman: Arthur Temple

TIME-LIFE BOOKS INC.
MANAGING EDITOR: Jerry Korn
Executive Editor: David Maness
Assistant Managing Editors: Dale M. Brown (planning),
George Constable, Jim Hicks (acting), Martin Mann,
John Paul Porter
Art Director: Tom Suzuki
Chief of Research: David L. Harrison
Director of Photography: Robert G. Mason
Senior Text Editor: Diana Hirsh
Assistant Art Director: Arnold C. Holeywell
Assistant Chief of Research: Carolyn L. Sackett
Assistant Director of Photography: Dolores A. Littles

CHAIRMAN: Joan D. Manley
President: John D. McSweeney
Executive Vice Presidents: Carl G. Jaeger,
John Steven Maxwell, David J. Walsh
Vice Presidents: Peter G. Barnes, Nicholas Benton
(public relations), John L. Canova (sales),
Nicholas J. C. Ingleton (Asia), James L. Mercer
(Europe/South Pacific), Herbert Sorkin (production),
Paul R. Stewart (promotion)
Personnel Director: Beatrice T. Dobie
Consumer Affairs Director: Carol Flaumenhaft

TIME-LIFE LIBRARY OF ART
EDITOR: Robert Morton
Editorial Staff for *The World of Picasso:*
Text Editor: Anne Horan
Picture Editor: Anthony Wolff
Designer: Paul Jensen
Assistant Designer: Leonard Wolfe
Staff Writers: Marianna Kastner, Frank Kendig,
James MaHood
Chief Researcher: Martha T. Goolrick
Researchers: Adrian Condon, Susan Grafman,
Martha Robson, Kelly Tasker, Yvonne Wong
Art Assistant: Nancy Earle

EDITORIAL PRODUCTION
Production Editor: Douglas B. Graham
Operations Manager: Gennaro C. Esposito,
Gordon E. Buck (assistant)
Assistant Production Editor: Feliciano Madrid
Quality Control: Robert L. Young (director),
James J. Cox (assistant), Michael G. Wight (associate)
Art Coordinator: Anne B. Landry
Copy Staff: Susan B. Galloway (chief), Muriel Clarke,
Celia Beattie
Picture Department: Joan T. Lynch
Traffic: Jeanne Potter

About the Author

Lael Wertenbaker is a former correspondent for TIME and LIFE who met Picasso toward the end of World War II. She wrote the widely acclaimed *Death of a Man*, the agonizing story of her husband's struggle against cancer. The book was turned into a Broadway play, *A Gift of Time*, by Garson Kanin. Her other books include *The Afternoon Women*, *Lament for Four Virgins* and *The Eye of the Lion*.

The Consulting Editor

H. W. Janson is Professor of Fine Arts at New York University. Among his numerous publications are his *History of Art* and *The Sculpture of Donatello*.

The Consultants for This Book

Sir Roland Penrose is a British Surrealist artist and art critic. As Chairman of the Institute of Contemporary Arts in London he has done much to promote the work of new artists. He was a close friend of Picasso's for over 30 years, and his works include the definitive study, *Picasso: His Life and Work*.

Robert Rosenblum taught in the Department of Art and Archeology at Princeton University between 1956 and 1966 and has been a guest professor at Yale and Columbia universities. He is now Professor of Fine Arts at New York University. His works include numerous articles on Picasso and his contemporaries, and the book *Cubism and Twentieth-Century Art*.

Slipcase

Picasso's portrait of his young son Paulo in a clown suit was painted in 1924.

End Papers

Four etchings on the subject of the artist and his model are part of a collection of 100 made on commission for the art dealer and publisher Ambroise Vollard.

CORRESPONDENTS: Elisabeth Kraemer (Bonn); Margot Hapgood, Dorothy Bacon, Lesley Coleman (London); Susan Jonas, Lucy T. Voulgaris (New York); Maria Vincenza Aloisi, Josephine du Brusle (Paris); Ann Natanson (Rome). Valuable assistance was also provided by the following individuals: Andrés Merce Varela (Barcelona); Robert Kroon, Alex des Fontaines (Geneva); Barbara Moir (London); Jean Bratton (Madrid); Peter Young (Moscow); Carolyn T. Chubet, Miriam Hsia, Zenona Green (New York).

Sixth printing. Revised 1980.
Published simultaneously in Canada.
Library of Congress catalogue card number 67-30587.
School and library distribution by Silver Burdett Company, Morristown, New Jersey.

Contents

I

The Spanish Prodigy

For more than three decades the dominant figure in Western art was a small muscular Spaniard who until his death at 91 exuded vitality. The genius of Pablo Picasso, probably the most prolific artist of all time, expressed itself with equal virtuosity in painting, drawing, sculpture, graphics and ceramics—and in enough of a variety of styles to have come from half a dozen men. He produced innovations that shocked, then saw his ideas established as canon. He influenced artists in every medium to which he put his hand—and architects as well, although theirs is a field he did not challenge directly.

Picasso's career spanned the entire course of modern art. In his youth, the imprint of Manet and the Impressionists was still fresh; their great successors, Gauguin and Van Gogh and Cézanne, were forging new paths. Picasso's own artistic coming of age coincided with the rise of other brilliant talents, among them Matisse and Braque and Rouault, who would make their mark on 20th Century painting. As the century progressed, spawning such diverse styles as Fauvism, Expressionism, Cubism, Futurism and Surrealism, Picasso was increasingly involved, often as prime mover and later as philosopher-sage. He lived to see perhaps the most momentous development of all: the transfer of the world's art capital from his beloved Paris to New York.

Even among people with little or no knowledge of art Picasso's name is familiar. American soldiers on leave in Paris at the end of World War II rated him with the Eiffel Tower among the sights they most wanted to see. As a consequence, an astonished Red Cross, with Picasso's consent, arranged tours of his studio. Those who met him, before he closed his door to be able to resume work, saw a short but well-built man with brilliant black eyes that seemed to pierce through whatever attracted his notice. Picasso's eyes were unforgettable; they rarely blinked, and often opened uncommonly wide, reflecting like polished dark mirrors the image they were intent upon. It is surely more than coincidence that eyes are a peculiar hallmark of his art. He painted and drew thousands of them in a thousand forms: with the exactitude of a photograph, or as crosses and dots, or in the shapes of birds, boats or beetles. He placed them any-

Picasso's father, Don José Ruiz Blasco *(above)*, demonstrated the ancestral streak of stubbornness that was to be so noticeable in his son when he defied tradition by rejecting his family's choice of a suitable bride. Although he liked the girl, he abruptly decided to marry her cousin. María Picasso López *(below)* became Picasso's mother.

where, one sideways and one lengthwise in a face, or hung under an ear behind glasses, or implanted in a forehead—anywhere, anyhow. Yet all of Picasso's eyes see.

Picasso's personality was as many-faceted as his achievements. He combined insatiable curiosity with a reluctance to dwell on anything that did not serve his art; reticence with sociability; elaborate courtesy with moody neglect; a yearning for attention with a demand for privacy. He had a flair for the unorthodox, a freedom of thought and behavior, and a personal dynamism that evoked widespread response.

As a shield against the avid interest he aroused, Picasso secluded himself in a villa at Mougins, a hilltop town near Cannes on the French Riviera. There he lived in an atmosphere of warm domesticity with his second wife, Jacqueline, some 40 years his junior, who openly adored him. He reigned over his domain like an absolute monarch. He received only those whom it pleased him to receive. When he did give of his time —to a grandchild, an old friend or a special stranger—he could be the quintessential Spanish host, wholly absorbed in the comfort of his guest. He was as jealous of his work as he was of his time; he sold only what he felt like selling and withheld whatever he chose.

In his tenth decade he continued to create. Almost every day, wearing a T-shirt and shorts or paint-splashed trousers, he disappeared into one of the few rooms of his large house that were not yet stacked to the ceiling with canvases and worked at his art. This was a major daily ritual, and one that he performed throughout his life from the time he was two. He preferred to work in solitude, but intimates sometimes watched him when he was unaware of their presence. When he was deeply involved with a canvas, his concentration was so intense that nothing could penetrate the invisible wall that seemed to enclose him and his easel. Jaime Sabartés, his lifelong friend and biographer, wrote that when Picasso painted the silence was so complete that the brush could be heard moving across the canvas.

Picasso was born on October 25, 1881, in the city of Málaga, in the region of Andalusia on the southern coast of Spain. The circumstances of his birth were decidedly inauspicious. He failed to breathe and the midwife abandoned him as stillborn. As Picasso tells the story, an uncle who was a doctor happened to be on hand and saved his life by blowing cigar smoke in his nose. Then, Picasso says, "I made a face and began to cry."

Two weeks later he was baptized Pablo Diego José Francisco de Paula Juan Nepomuceno María de los Remedios Cipriano de la Santísima Trinidad—a roster of names that honored various godparents, relatives and saints. At the end of this long string came two more names, Ruiz and Picasso—the first for his father and the second for his mother, as is Spanish custom. As a young artist Picasso would sign himself P. Ruiz or P. Ruiz Picasso until about 1902, when he settled on Picasso alone—partly because it was less common than Ruiz, partly out of fondness for his mother.

Picasso's family belonged to the professional middle class. His father, Don José Ruiz Blasco, whose forebears had been minor aristocrats, was a tall man nicknamed "the Englishman" because of his reddish hair and his liking for English ways. He was a museum curator, a teacher of art and an artist. Picasso once described his father's paintings as "dining room pictures, the kind with partridges and pigeons, hares and rabbits, fur and feather. Fowl and flowers. Especially pigeons and lilies. Lilies and pigeons."

Don José's eldest brother, Picasso's Uncle Diego, was a diplomat who once served as an envoy to Russia. Another uncle, Pablo, was a doctor of theology and canon of the cathedral in Málaga. The third, Salvador, the cigar-smoking doctor who rescued Picasso at birth, was Director of the Health Department of the Port of Málaga.

Picasso inherited his looks from his mother, María Picasso López, a petite Malagueña with coal black hair, the daughter of a civil servant who went to Cuba when she was a child and disappeared there. The name Picasso is found in Italy as well as in Spain, and María's grandfather is known to have been born in a village near Genoa; thus it is possible, as many biographers have asserted, that she was somehow related to Matteo Picasso, a Genoese artist of the mid-19th Century. Her son discounted this theory, but he was interested enough in it to have purchased a portrait painted by Matteo Picasso.

Other biographers, hoping to explain the calligraphic flourishes that Picasso often employed in his drawings, have tried to trace his ancestry to the Moors, and still others to the gypsies, because he was quick to turn any place he inhabited into a camp, and was prone to regard the world with a bright amoral stare. Genealogy supports neither claim, but insofar as both the gypsies and the Moors are a part of the mainstream of Spanish culture, both have contributed to Picasso's heritage.

Picasso seldom reminisced about his childhood, but when in the mood to talk about it he spoke in singular detail. Remembering some 50 years later an earthquake from which his family fled when he was three, Picasso told Sabartés: "My mother was wearing a kerchief on her head. I had never seen her like that before. My father took his cape from the rack, threw it over himself, took me in his arms and wound me in its folds." Another time, delighted with sudden recall, he exclaimed: "I remember I learned to walk by pushing a tin of Olibet biscuits because I knew what was inside."

Apparently he could draw before he could talk. His first words, according to his mother, were "piz, piz" for *lápiz*, the Spanish for pencil —an object he was always demanding. Often he covered entire sheets of paper with elaborate spirals, which, he managed to indicate to admiring relatives, were *torruellas*—spun sugar cakes, whose name derives from a word meaning "to bewilder or entangle." The spiral form of the *torruellas* would recur in his work years later, transformed, for example, into breasts in a portrait of one of his mistresses.

Like many another parent of a prodigy, Picasso's father encouraged and disciplined him in his precocity. Don José was giving Pablo serious instruction in art by the time he was seven. The boy took to it readily. He was, in fact, preoccupied with art; he swore that he never knew the sequence of the alphabet and that he received a grammar school

F. MARTIN. Plaza del Teatro, 56. MALAGA

Details of the past remain sharp in Picasso's precise visual memory. When, at the age of 74, he was shown this black-and-white photograph of himself taken at the age of four, he was able to recall the exact color of the clothes he had worn at the time: a vermilion jacket with gold buttons, bronze-colored shoes, a white bow and collar.

certificate only because a kindly Málaga schoolmaster supplied him with the answers he required to pass an arithmetic test.

As a budding artist Picasso took his inspiration from subjects at hand. Some of his earliest drawings were of pigeons, which his father kept to use as models for his own painting, and of the animals that roamed the streets of Málaga. He was so proficient at sketching that he could start from any point—the belly of a horse or the tail of a burro—and in one continuous line produce a remarkable likeness of the beast. He could also cut their forms unerringly from paper with little scissors. Birds and animals delighted him even in the Cold War era, when a Picasso "dove of peace" served Communist propagandists on millions of posters.

Young Pablo had another ready subject in the bullfights, which he began attending while small enough to be admitted free because he could sit on his father's lap. The first oil he ever attempted, painted on wood when he was eight or nine, shows some people watching a picador in the bullring. He kept the painting until his death, although it was somewhat damaged; Picasso's younger sister, Lola, then aged five or six, had poked nails through the eyes. His first etching, made on copperplate when he was 17, was also of a picador. He failed to anticipate that the image would be reversed in printing, and when he saw the result, with the picador holding the lance in his left hand, he blandly titled it *El Zurdo (The Left-handed One)*. By then he was living in Barcelona and was soon to be celebrated among his friends for his marvelous re-creations of the bullfights there. "People think that I painted the pictures of bullfights in those days after they were over," he once said. "Not at all. I painted them the day before and sold them to anyone so as to have enough money to buy a ticket."

Picasso's lifelong absorption in bullfights, his use of the monochromatic browns and ochers peculiar to the Spanish landscape, his love of the grotesque, his concern with the real even when painting at his most obscure (by his own word, he regarded himself as above all a realist)—all these were indisputably in the tradition of Spanish painting. Despite the fact that he lived in France for more than two thirds of his life, Picasso

Pigeons were a favorite subject of Picasso's from his earliest years. The birds were kept by his father as subjects for his own painting and flew freely through the family rooms. Even some 50 years later, Picasso enjoyed having them fly about his studio in Paris. Young Pablo made this drawing when he was only 11, but it already shows his freedom of line within a very controlled composition.

remained thoroughly Spanish, both in his work and in his moods of *sol y sombra*—sun and shade. When he spoke Spanish, his whole manner lightened, and his gestures quickened.

In 1891, when Picasso was almost 10, his father took a teaching post at the School of Fine Arts in La Coruña, an Atlantic port 700 miles northwest of Málaga where for part of the year rain and fog replaced the warmth and luminous horizon to which the family had been accustomed. Away from Andalusia, Picasso recalled, his father grew morose and listless. Much of the time he sat watching the rain through the window, and he seldom painted. When he did, he usually left the work unfinished, then turned it over to his son to complete for him.

One evening Don José returned from a stroll to find that Pablo had taken one of his unfinished sketches—of a pigeon—and painted with exquisite precision the talons and the delicate feathering along the bird's legs. The effect was better than anything the father himself had ever achieved. Ambivalently gripped with pride and despair, Don José handed his own palette and brushes to his son, then 13, and vowed never to paint again.

When Picasso was not painting, or at school, or sitting in on his father's classes, he walked everywhere, searching the world around him for subjects. In short order he filled a great many sketchbooks with drawings of the harbor of La Coruña, the beach and the surrounding countryside, as well as with numerous portraits of his sister Lola. Always he worked without hesitation, capturing images with incredible speed and rarely altering what he had done.

For his relatives in distant Málaga, Picasso issued a miniature news sheet to which he gave various journalistic titles such as *La Coruña* and *Azul y Blanco (Blue and White)*—the latter probably a play on the name of a well-known Spanish magazine, *Blanco y Negro (White and Black)*. The "Director, P. Ruiz," as he proclaimed himself on the masthead, also served as editor, writer, reporter, layout man and artist. The illustrations were topical, often touching on La Coruña's dismal weather. Under a drawing of a man gripping his umbrella in a downpour he wrote: "The rain has begun, and will continue until summer." An adjacent drawing of two men and a woman whipped by the wind is captioned: "Also, the wind has begun and will continue until Coruña is no more." These sketches, executed with total self-assurance, reveal both a grasp of anatomy and a talent for lifelike detail.

Years later, in 1946, Picasso visited an exhibition of British and French children's art and commented that at their age he was drawing like Raphael, that "it took me many years to learn how to draw like these children." He whose sense of freedom brought about a revolution in art served an apprenticeship rigidly bound by tradition. This was his father's doing. Like all run-of-the-mill instructors of his time, Don José felt strongly that the best training for a young painter consisted first of assiduously copying the masters, then drawing from plaster casts of the human body and from live models. The aim was to produce exact likenesses, and the student who could not do so was believed to have no future as a painter. Such an approach left little room for imagination

This drawing of Christ administering Grace to the Devil was made by Picasso at the age of 14. He had used it as an illustration for an issue of a small family newspaper he had created for Christmas Day, 1895. Picasso jokingly showed it to a visitor 62 years later as an example of "early church art." The drawing spilled out of an old leather portfolio that was crammed with copies of other little handmade newspapers and numerous sketches Picasso had made between 1888 and 1895.

or originality—not only in Spain but in academic art circles everywhere.

The Ruiz family remained in La Coruña for nearly four years, until 1895, when a professor at the School of Fine Arts in Barcelona offered to trade positions with Don José. Never reconciled to La Coruña, Don José leaped at the chance. The family's move was preceded by a visit to Málaga, where the relatives made a great fuss over Pablo, already, at 13, regarded as the family genius. Uncle Salvador paid models to pose for his nephew. One was an old sailor whose realistic portrait displayed Picasso's extraordinary draftsmanship. Pablo's eccentric Aunt Pepa also sat for him; though the day was blazing, she insisted on wearing her fur coat and all her jewels.

When Picasso first saw Barcelona it was—as it is today—Spain's most cosmopolitan city. Despite its warm sunshine and equable temperatures, its energetic citizens considered themselves northerners. They regarded their fellow countrymen to the south, the Andalusians, as feckless and lazy. Fiercely proud of their city as a wellspring of Spanish culture, they clung, then as now, to their own language, Catalan—like Spanish, an offshoot of Latin.

Situated on the Mediterranean, Barcelona has been a crossroads of East and West since the rise of medieval commerce. Heart of the region of Catalonia, it has shared in an illustrious history. From the 13th Century to the 15th—and prior to the reign of Ferdinand and Isabella, who brought the provinces that today constitute Spain under centralized rule—the Catalans enjoyed political independence, economic prosperity and a flourishing art. Now, in the 1890s, they were preoccupied with *modernismo*, an intellectual movement that deplored the materialism brought on by industrial advance. Its ideas had filtered in from the north of Europe: from the works of Friedrich Nietzsche and Arthur Schopenhauer in Germany, from Maurice Maeterlinck in Belgium, from the Pre-Raphaelites in England. In Barcelona its leading exponent was the architect Antoni Gaudí, a defiant individualist who, in his buildings, rejected traditional ideas of symmetry and flat surfaces in favor of "natural" curves and billows. Politics and letters concerned adherents of *modernismo* no less than the arts. Some venerated the past and urged a reassertion of ancient or medieval values. Others advocated the overthrow of all tradition and established order in favor of anarchy, in the arts and in politics alike. With these contradictions in mind Jaime Brossa, an eminent local philosopher, once remarked that listening to an argument in a Barcelona café was like hearing a Chopin ballade and *The Marseillaise* played simultaneously.

Whether favoring modern anarchism or medieval order, political talk centered on separatism; Catalans, partly because of their distinctive language, partly because of their history, believed that Catalonia should sever its formal ties with Madrid and the rest of Spain. In art the view prevailed that, with the 20th Century approaching, artists were on the threshold of a great new day and some great new style.

All the artistic ferment and talk of *modernismo* escaped Don José, who was scarcely happier in Barcelona than he had been in La Coruña. But his son thrived in the new surroundings and became so identified

Drawing and painting in the academic fashion—occasionally from live models but most often from plaster casts—the young Picasso worked under his father's vigilant tutelage. The training was rigidly traditional. He made faithful copies of the dreary busts and torsos in the art school at La Coruña, where, because his father was on the faculty, he was able to spend his days.

with Barcelona that many people, even Spaniards, believed that he was born there. Picasso's friends say that when he suffered, as he often did, from *morriña*—a term that encompasses both the blues and nostalgia—it was for Barcelona, which he regarded as his true home.

Soon after the family settled down, Don José decided it was time that Pablo undertook the formal study of art. As a faculty member at the School of Fine Arts—better known as La Lonja from the trading exchange in which it was housed—Don José could pull some special strings. He persuaded school officials to allow his son to take the examination for entry into the advanced class, which was meant for students far more mature than Pablo. The examination required two charcoal drawings of a living model, to be strictly judged for realism and precision. Picasso finished the task in a week, a quarter of the time most students took. Both drawings are still in the school archives. An awed jury admitted the 13-year-old candidate to the school forthwith. Once enrolled, he left something to be desired in his attention to discipline, but he made several fast friends—among them Manuel Pallarés, Manuel Hugué, Sebastián Junyer-Vidal and Carles Casagemas, all of whom were to figure in his later life.

In time, Don José rented a tiny room near home where the boy could work in solitude. But like many another father, he was loath to let go. Four or five times a day, en route to and from his classes at La Lonja, he dropped in at the new studio, and he persisted in marking Pablo's drawings "Failed" or "Distinguished," as it suited him. His son soon balked under this surveillance and arguments between the two began to be frequent.

At 15 Picasso won honorable mention at the periodic National Exhibition of Fine Arts in Madrid for *Science and Charity*, a painting of a sick woman attended by a doctor and a nun. The extreme elongation of the woman's hands prompted the art critic of a Madrid newspaper to scoff that the doctor—for whom Don José had served as a model—was taking "the pulse of a glove." Not all critics shared this derisive view, however. The same picture later won a gold medal in a local competition in Málaga.

Eventually Don José and Uncle Salvador decided Pablo should attend the Royal Academy of San Fernando in Madrid, the foremost art school in Spain; a century earlier the great Goya, cherished by all Spaniards, had been the director of painting there. In 1897, with the promise of an allowance from Uncle Salvador, Picasso set off for the capital—barely 16 and, for the first time, on his own.

No doubt Picasso meant to attend the academy in Madrid, but he tended to chafe under any kind of formal instruction and so, asserting his now-famous instinct for independence, he stopped going to classes soon after he had enrolled. But he was not idle. Madrid, with its contrasts of wealth and poverty, its broad boulevards and squalid alleys, endlessly fascinated him and spurred him to work at almost fever pitch. Not the least of Madrid's attractions was the Prado, with its glorious collections of paintings by Velázquez, Goya, Zurbarán and others. Perhaps above all Picasso admired the work of El Greco, who had fallen out

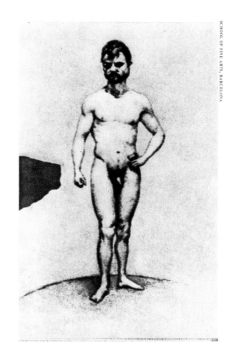

This unflatteringly realistic nude study was made by Picasso in 1895 as part of his entrance examination to an art school in Barcelona. The jury, believing they had discovered a prodigy, swiftly admitted him. Although his teachers considered his drawings to be extraordinarily mature, Picasso later confided to his friend Kahnweiler that he much preferred the pictures he had done earlier, perhaps because they were much more spontaneous.

Pablo Picasso

Ramón Casas

J. M. Soler

of fashion after his death in 1614 because his jarring colors, his anti-realism and the eccentrically elongated limbs and mystical faces of his subjects were thought to flout Spanish tradition. Picasso sent his father pictures which he painted in conscious imitation of El Greco, and Don José wrote back: "You are following the bad way."

Although this was a prolific period for Picasso, little has survived from it. Uncle Salvador cut off funds when he learned that his protégé was shunning school, and the occasional sums sent by Don José were so small that Picasso was too poor to buy much drawing paper, let alone canvas. The few pieces of paper that remain are crowded to the edges with sketches of bourgeois citizens, gypsies, beggars and café scenes.

In the spring of 1898 Picasso came down with scarlet fever, decided he had had enough of Madrid and left. With Manuel Pallarés, his first friend at La Lonja, he went to recuperate in Horta de San Juan—a village in Catalonia that Picasso called "Horta de Ebro," after its river.

This was his first encounter with country life. A child of the city, he already knew and sympathized with the lot of the urban downtrodden, caught up in a way of life whose material benefits they did not share; now he began to understand the human struggle against the forces of nature. Irrigation made the Ebro valley rich, but beyond the valley the landscape stretched to a forbidding horizon of limestone mountains. Peasants lived huddled together in stone houses and fought for survival with their bare hands. Despite the harshness of the life, Picasso loved it. He learned to yoke oxen, load mules and milk cows; later he would boast of his proficiency. Working alongside the villagers at their tasks, he made numerous sketches of them, all tranquil scenes that reflect his peace of mind.

He returned to Barcelona in the spring of 1899, a healthy and exuberant 17-year-old fully prepared for adulthood. His essential character was formed, the pattern of his life plainly set. He could be ruthless or gentle, gregarious or withdrawn. He combined prankish gaiety with a sense of human tragedy, moods of elation with moods of black despair. Acutely sensitive, he was open to all manner of ideas—but on his own terms, for he was too ruggedly independent to submit to the dominance of others.

He wholeheartedly adopted the city and everything it had to offer—and the city embraced him in return. Young as he was, he proved to be a natural catalyst, for he radiated an intensity that charged the atmosphere around him. He listened more than he talked, had a sharp wit that delighted more than it offended, and a cocky masculinity that intrigued women. Before long he was the favorite of a Bohemian set that met nightly at the tavern Els Quatre Gats—Catalan for "The Four Cats." The name was a variation on Le Chat Noir, a Montmartre café, and was also based on a Catalan saying, "We're only four cats," meaning "There's nobody here of any account." At Els Quatre Gats *modernismo* was the main topic of conversation; it was the theme of two successive reviews published by Pere Romeu, the café owner. Paintings by young unknowns decorated the walls, and the café was also the scene of puppet shows and shadow plays directed by Miguel Utrillo, the art historian who was later to adopt the painter Maurice Utrillo as his son.

Picasso no longer lived at home, but shared a series of studios with other impecunious artists. Each place became his own, cluttered with his sketches, canvases, paints and brushes. Financed only by a pittance from his father, he lived from hand to mouth. But he managed to make occasional small sales of his sketches to *modernismo* reviews—to Romeu's *Pél i Ploma (Brush and Pen)*, to *Joventut (Youth)*, and to *Catalunya Artística*. He also filled cheap sketchbooks with studies of his friends, the Barcelona docks, dance halls, cabarets and brothels, the rooftops from his garret window, and, of course, the bullfights.

His abiding affection for his family, whom he visited daily, showed in portraits of Lola and Don José and in a number of conventional pictures on conventional themes that he painted solely to please his father. But in much of his work Picasso was beginning to reflect change. Miguel Utrillo introduced him to the work of Jaime Huguet, a 15th Century Catalan primitive, and rekindled his enthusiasm for El Greco. He also met a local painter, Ramón Casas, who encouraged him to emulate the stark realism of the Swiss lithographer Théophile Alexandre Steinlen and the Post-Impressionist Henri de Toulouse-Lautrec. The capacity for spongelike absorption that characterized Picasso from that time began to be apparent. He used the attenuated figures of El Greco, the strong colors and bold strokes of Toulouse-Lautrec, and sometimes the two-dimensional figures of Japanese prints, then a vogue all over Europe. Whatever his choice of styles, he displayed one significant consistency: invariably, he depicted his subjects with compassion.

It was, in sum, a fertile and meaningful period for Picasso. In February 1900 he had his first exhibition at Els Quatre Gats and his first favorable press notice. The anonymous critic—thought to have been a professor at La Lonja—wrote that the artist, "hardly more than a child," showed "extraordinary facility in the use of brush and pencil." He also noted the diversity of influences acting upon Picasso. Most of the drawings on display were portraits of Picasso's friends.

Despite the stimulation of Barcelona, he began to be restless. He thought of going to England. Don José had mixed feelings about the idea. Dour and friendless, still melancholy away from Andalusia, he was reluctant to part with his son; he lived only for the boy's art. But he had always dreamed of seeing London himself, and no doubt he hoped that the works of the great English portrait painters would inspire his son. So he handed over all the money he could scrape together—without telling Picasso how bare this left the family cupboard—to finance the English venture.

In the fall of 1900 Picasso set off for London with Carles Casagemas, his classmate from La Lonja, with whom he had been sharing a studio. On the way they stopped in Paris. Several of their friends had preceded them, in line with the belief, held in Barcelona as elsewhere, that all artists and dressmakers must go to Paris. Picasso was about to experience some of the best years of his life. Although only 19, he could look back upon a sizable body of work that was varied and assured. Now he was to test his talents in the world's greatest arena of art.

Santiago Rusiñol

Ramón Pitxot

Fujolá y Vallés

Pere Romeu

In Search of a Style

Even as a child Picasso was a formidable draftsman and by the time he was 14, when he made the portrait at right, he had become a competent painter as well. Technical virtuosity came so easily to him that at 16, after having studied in several art schools, he quickly lost interest in academic training, with its rigid emphasis on copying and severely limited subject matter. What did fascinate him was the life of the city; scenes of the cafés, sketches of the poor and drawings of street entertainers flowed from his hand.

In his own search for a personal means of expression, Picasso turned away from the art of the academy and joined the revolution brewing in Paris and other northern cities since the 1870s, when the Impressionists established their colorful technique. He was intrigued by their work and also by the expressive style of later innovators like Toulouse-Lautrec, Van Gogh and Gauguin, which he knew only by description or reproductions. He drew support for his own work from the fact that their subject matter—city life—was the very one he had chosen.

By the time he was 19, Picasso had left home in search of the action in art, which he knew was outside Spain. Although he returned there three times during the next few years, it became clear that Paris was to be home. Before he was 25, he had wrought his great natural abilities into a powerful, personal style—the first that could unmistakably be called "Picasso."

Treasured by Picasso as a favorite early work, this portrait of an impoverished girl was painted from a live model before he entered art school. Already he was so skillful that the girl's body and face—and even her intense gaze— are rendered with great confidence.

Girl with Bare Feet, 1895

17

The Altar Boy, 1896

Don José Ruiz Blasco: *The Pigeons*, c.1889

Honoré Daumier, *The Follies of Paris*, 1863

Picasso's first teacher was his father, Don José Ruiz Blasco, a skilled painter of traditional subjects like the one above at the left. Don José's teaching method was academic, and under his direction his son learned to paint with meticulous accuracy. The picture at left reveals his technical skill in the careful proportions of the figure and the precise delineation of the altar boy's delicate lace surplice. Yet even this early work hints at the originality that was to mark the rest of his career, for Picasso simplified the scene, eliminating much of the background that a traditional painter would have crowded into the picture.

Picasso first fully broke away from his father's tradition with a scene depicting a dingy tavern interior *(below)*, a work influenced by Daumier lithographs like the one above at right. Not only in its real-life subject, a change from the posed scenes of home and church he had been doing, but in its rough brushwork, heavy outlines and muddy colors, this youthful painting foreshadows the expressive style Picasso would develop.

Tavern Interior, 1897

Poster for Els Quatre Gats (The Four Cats), 189

Henri de Toulouse-Lautrec: Poster, 1896

Pierre-Auguste Renoir: *Le Moulin de la Galette*, 1876

In his late teens Picasso became involved with the artistic avant-garde of Barcelona. Headquarters for the intellectuals was a café called Els Quatre Gats, where talk often turned to the great artists who were working in London and Paris. One of their favorites was Toulouse-Lautrec, whose expressive posters *(left, above)* for cafés, dance halls and theaters had reached a wide audience. In a poster *(far left)* that he designed for his café, Picasso shows the Frenchman's influence unmistakably in his use of bright colors and sinuous, heavily outlined shapes.

Despite the excitement in Barcelona, Picasso wanted to see the advances in art being made elsewhere. At the age of 19, he set out for London, but stopped over in Paris and got no farther. The first oil painting he did there *(below)* was a scene at the café Le Moulin de la Galette, a Montmartre landmark made famous by earlier painters. But the atmosphere had changed since the time when Renoir painted the sunny scene at the left. Its gay middle-class patrons are replaced in Picasso's picture by a bored and garish-looking clientele given a faintly decadent glow by the illumination of gas lamps.

Le Moulin de la Galette, 1900

Dwarf Dancer, 1901

During Picasso's stay in Paris he rapidly assimilated varied painting techniques. When he returned to Spain, he combined them with typically Spanish subjects. The quick, flickering brush strokes of pure color that float like clouds in parts of these two pictures are characteristic of painters like the Impressionists Claude Monet and Pierre-Auguste Renoir. But in their brilliantly colored works they had been concerned primarily with capturing the evanescent effects of light. Picasso was also interested in evoking a heightened emotional tone. His bold blocks of color, brushed on in crude, energetic strokes, create a strong sense of drama.

Picasso's Spanish heritage shows through vividly in both paintings. The bullfight is a subject to which he

22

Bullfight, 1901

returned often, and the pathetic dying horse foreshadows a powerful image that would appear more than 30 years later in his brilliant painting *Guernica (page 137).* The picture at the left above shows Picasso's sense of identity with the tradition of Spanish art. The figure was inspired by one in a painting by the 17th Century master Velázquez. *Las Meninas* shows a princess, her attendants and dwarf entertainer, and is among the finest Spanish pictures of all time *(page 160).* But Picasso did not imitate Velázquez; he simply borrowed his subject. A friend recalls that the artist came into Els Quatre Gats with his picture and a reproduction of the Velázquez, laid them side by side, and said proudly, "Velázquez did *that*; Picasso did *that*."

23

When Picasso returned to Paris after six months in Spain his style was still derivative. He continued to experiment with the techniques of others, most notably Van Gogh and Gauguin. Instinctively, it seems, the Spaniard was attracted to painters whose strong colors, expressive line and clear indication of mood and feeling were close to his own sense of what painting should be.

In his portrait of Manyac *(below)*, the dealer who had been providing him with a monthly stipend in return for his output, Picasso owes a debt to Gauguin; the bright fields of color separated by sharp outlines recall those of Gauguin's own self-portrait *(bottom)*. Picasso's *Harlequin (right)* shows not only Gauguin's influence but that of Van Gogh as well. The pose of the Harlequin is strikingly similar to that of Van Gogh's picture of a pensive woman below. But Picasso has begun to express his individuality in this picture, for there are subtle nuances here that create a new mood quite unlike Van Gogh's. The introspective gaze of the Harlequin and Picasso's use of cool tones create a strong sense of isolation and dejection.

Pere Manyac, 1901

Vincent Van Gogh: *The Arlesienne*, 1888

Paul Gauguin: *Self-Portrait*, 1889

Harlequin, 1901

The pervasive blue that floods this moody picture is a characteristic that would dominate Picasso's work for the next three years—a time known as his Blue Period. The picture, painted in 1901, gives the first indication that he would adopt such an unusual, distinctively personal stylization, but it also reveals that his debt to other painters was still strong.

The subject itself, a nude woman bathing in a room, had been a favorite of Degas and Renoir, who painted dozens of such intimate scenes. Picasso pays homage to Toulouse-Lautrec, his earlier inspiration, by showing a vaguely defined copy of a Lautrec painting hanging on the wall above the bed. To the left of the Lautrec is a seaside scene that could be by either Monet or Gauguin.

In the end, though, the painting is much more than a sum of its creator's indebtedness to the past. In its downcast emotional tone, in its roughly brushed, crude but expressive rendering of the human figure, and in its sense of quietude and isolation, *The Blue Room* stands as the product of a full-fledged artist—one who was to assert himself even more strongly in the years to come.

The Blue Room, 1901

28

II

"La Bande à Picasso"

The first time Picasso saw Paris the city was basking in the golden age known as *la belle époque*. Trade and colonialism had poured unprecedented wealth into Europe; industrialization had multiplied material comforts; and a whole generation had come of age untouched by war. The rich put on a dazzling show, dressing extravagantly, dining lavishly at Maxim's, flaunting their infidelities. The painter Maurice de Vlaminck recalled in his memoirs that at the turn of the century "half of Paris seemed to be perpetually strolling round with a little cash in its pockets." But the scene had its seamy side. Behind the glittering façade of high society, workers toiled at least 10 hours a day for a pittance and beggars haunted the streets.

The arts existed amid similar contradictions. Academic painters held fast to prescriptions for composition, perspective and color that had ruled art since the Renaissance. But an artistic revolution had been gathering force ever since the 1860s, when Édouard Manet first shattered certain Renaissance conventions. He dared to paint the female nude in everyday settings rather than as an idealized Venus, and he all but abandoned *chiaroscuro*, the modeling of figures by the use of light and shade. One appalled older painter denounced a work by Manet on the grounds that its people were "as flat as the figures on playing cards."

Manet's innovations withstood attack, and the artists who followed him took further liberties with both technique and subject matter. The Impressionists of the 1870s disregarded conventional modeling altogether, and instead aimed at capturing the ephemeral effects of light. They used bright colors instead of the somber hues of the traditional masters, and a new kind of dappled brushwork of small, quick strokes.

Manet and the Impressionists drew on the world around them for themes, without moralizing—a recent tradition founded by a group of Realists of the mid-19th Century. Subsequent artists, instead of literally reproducing nature, strove to express their personal sensations. Vincent Van Gogh chose his colors for their emotional impact. Paul Gauguin emulated the simplicity of primitive art. Paul Cézanne established a new concept of form in his painting, altering the accepted

One of Picasso's first self-portraits in oils, this picture was painted during his second sojourn in Paris when he was only 20. His drawn face and scraggly beard attest to the youthful Bohemian's hard life—he had as yet achieved no success. But his intense gaze reveals his determination. The blue cast of this picture fits the somber mood.

Self-Portrait, 1901

29

appearance of objects by warping apples into imperfect spheres and tabletops into imperfect rectangles.

While some artists turned toward simplification, others took the opposite path toward elaborate ornamentation. This new style, called Art Nouveau, had its roots in a belief that craftsmanship had gone out of art. Its practitioners first applied it in architecture, printing and interior design, later in painting. They looked for inspiration to Celtic ornament and Medieval tracery, to Japanese prints and Javanese textiles. They also made much use of natural forms, although they sometimes exaggerated them almost to the point of caricature by means of an intricate, serpentine line; there were no counterparts in nature for the peacocks' tails and lily pads that adorned their vases and lampshades.

Although few major painters counted themselves part of Art Nouveau, its spirit affected them all. That spirit was summed up by the Munich architect August Endell: "We stand at the threshold of an altogether new art, an art with forms which mean or represent nothing, yet which can stimulate our souls as deeply as the sounds of music have been able to do." The excitement of taking part in a new art aborning which dominated Europe at the turn of the century infected the 19-year-old Picasso when he arrived in Paris in October 1900.

Sinuous curves and sweeping floral patterns characterize the turn-of-the-century style known as Art Nouveau. It influenced painting and had a strong effect on the decorative arts —the lily pad windows *(above)* in Antoni Gaudí's Casa Milá apartment house in Barcelona and the tendril-like grillwork that Hector Guimard designed for a Paris subway entrance *(below)* are typical examples.

Picasso and his traveling companion, Carles Casagemas, were inevitably drawn to Montmartre, a quarter on the northern outskirts of the city where Bohemian artists of every nationality lived in crowded company with workingmen, tramps, circus performers and petty criminals. Situated on a butte high above the metropolis, Montmartre spread on terraced hillsides where windmills had turned and grapevines ripened not long before. Narrow cobbled streets and muddy alleys climbed precipitously between warrens of tenements that were freezing in winter and stifling in summer. For relief, the residents frequented cheap cafés and amusement halls where a few francs bought food, warmth and entertainment. In this rugged but friendly atmosphere Picasso soon forgot his plan to visit England. He became so popular in the Barcelona colony of Montmartre that in time the Spaniards came to be known in the neighborhood as *la bande à Picasso*—Picasso's crew.

He also found a place to work. The Catalan painter Isidre Nonell, who had decided to return home, gave him his studio, a room on the narrow Rue Gabrielle near the summit of Montmartre. Moreover, Picasso acquired a dealer, a Barcelonan named Pere Manyac, who offered him a monthly stipend of 150 francs—about $30—for all he could produce. Many a laborer lived on less; for Picasso the sum was enough to keep him in room and board, canvas and paint.

When he was not painting Picasso gorged himself on the free feast the city spread before his eyes. At the Louvre he saw the old masters revered by his father; at dealers' galleries he saw the works of the Impressionists and Post-Impressionists, which up to now he had known only through magazine reproductions. At night he patronized the cafés. And, as before, when he painted, he focused on the scene at hand, replacing the streets and cafés of Barcelona with those of Montmartre. Away from his father's supervisory eye, he broke loose from academic restraints. He brightened his palette with the luminous colors of the Impressionists and simplified the modeling of his figures. One of his best surviving works of the time is *Le Moulin de la Galette (page 21)*, in which the figures of men and women in a cabaret are dark and silhouetted against bright greens and oranges that seem to flicker like gaslight. Obviously he had taken a leaf from Toulouse-Lautrec.

He was happy in Paris, but he had promised his father to be home for Christmas. Besides, his friend Casagemas was miserable. Casagemas had fallen in love, been spurned and taken to drink. Worse, he talked of suicide. Picasso thought the Spanish sun might cure his friend's lovesickness, and together they headed back to Barcelona.

The homecoming was fraught with tension. Don José objected to the boys' appearance: their hair was long and shaggy, their dress Bohemian and bizarre. But chiefly he was dismayed by his son's new pictures; to the conventional Don José these Impressionistic daubings seemed a shameful waste of good talent.

After Christmas Picasso left for Málaga, taking Casagemas with him. The stay was no happier than in Barcelona. Uncle Salvador demanded that Picasso cut his hair and paint sensibly; there was money to be made in Spain by anyone with a talent for portraiture. To complicate matters, Casagemas grew more despondent. All day and night he sat in a bar drinking and listening gloomily to gypsies wail their *cante jondo*—Andalusian songs of heartbreak. Unable to help his friend, and made miserable by family recriminations, Picasso fled to Madrid.

There his spirits brightened when he found another friend from Barcelona, Francisco de Asís Soler, an anarchist bent on awakening the Spanish capital to Catalan *modernismo*. The two joined forces to publish a magazine called *Arte Joven (Young Art)*. Soler solicited articles from intellectuals and Picasso supplied the illustrations. Most were grimly realistic cartoons aimed at various social and political ills, and full of sympathy for the harsh lot of the poor. The magazine was short-lived; for lack of funds it expired after five issues.

In his preoccupation, Picasso had failed to live up to his agreement with the dealer Pere Manyac, who wrote demanding the works he had been promised. So toward the spring of 1901 Picasso packed a portfolio and set off again for Paris, stopping briefly in Barcelona to bid his family an uneasy farewell. He was beginning to be aware that the gulf between him and his father could never be bridged. The personal and artistic freedom he had tasted in Paris made it impossible for him to continue to accept Don José's counsel on painting, impossible to readjust to his strait-laced mores. Soon afterward Picasso underscored his differences with his father by dropping the Ruiz from his signature. From that time on his works bore only "Picasso," his mother's name.

In Paris Manyac gave Picasso one of the two rooms in his apartment in Montmartre and also unselfishly introduced him to another dealer, Ambroise Vollard. A tall man with a high, domed forehead, full cheeks and a tiny, pursed mouth, Vollard was endowed with an astute business sense and remarkable foresight. His friends argued hotly over whether he had superb taste or no taste in art, and sometimes the second view

Looking like an advertisement for "What the Well-Dressed Young Painter Should Wear," Picasso is nattily attired in knickerbockers and a broad-brimmed hat in this self-portrait drawn soon after his return to Paris in 1901. The bearded pipe smoker at the lower right is his companion on the trip, Jaumet Andreu Bonsons, a Catalan friend.

Max Jacob, Picasso's first French friend, masked his terrible poverty with a fine long coat, made by his tailor father, and a top hat, which he shared with Picasso. When Picasso went home to Barcelona in 1901 for want of money he sent Jacob a letter *(below)* with a sketch of himself. The letter complained that Picasso's Spanish friends criticized his work as having "too much soul and not enough form," a reference to the morbid emotionalism of his Blue Period paintings.

seemed borne out by the sight of Vollard dozing amid the dirt and clutter of his gallery. He was rude to prospective buyers and tough on the painters he promoted; Cézanne called him a "slave-driver." But the hard-headed Vollard was already well along toward acquiring a worldwide clientele of wealthy collectors and important museums.

On seeing Picasso's works, Vollard promptly offered him a showing, together with a Basque painter named Iturrino. For a 19-year-old, such sponsorship was an undeniable coup. Almost anything exhibited at Vollard's gallery was certain to attract critical notice. Thus Picasso elicited his first reviews in the Paris press. The critic Félicien Fagus wrote in *La Revue Blanche,* an avant-garde magazine: "Picasso is a painter, absolutely and beautifully. . . . He is in love with every subject and to him everything is a subject. . . . One can easily perceive many a probable influence apart from that of his own great ancestry: Delacroix, Manet, Monet, Van Gogh, Pissarro, Toulouse-Lautrec, Degas, Forain, Rops, others perhaps . . . each one a passing phase." Fagus concluded this perceptive summary by adding that Picasso's "passionate surge forward has not yet left him the leisure to forge for himself a personal style"—but this Picasso was soon to do.

During this second sojourn in Paris Picasso formed a lasting friendship with a young writer named Max Jacob. The son of a Jewish tailor and antique dealer in Brittany, Jacob had spent a cheerless childhood as a Jew in a Gentile society, and still suffered from a sense of stigma. His looks did not help; he was a little man with a large head, and his pince-nez and habitual top hat seemed somehow comic. Paradox personified, he perpetually wrestled with a sense of sin and a love of pleasure, a wish to conform and an urge to let loose. He could be stiffly formal at the start of a party, then devastate the room by pulling up his trouser legs to imitate a dancing girl. Like Picasso, he combined his love of nonsense with a deep melancholy, but unlike Picasso, who was already a pronounced skeptic, he was undergoing a spiritual crisis that would culminate in his conversion to Catholicism.

Jacob saw Picasso's exhibition at Vollard's and by his own account was "struck with wonder." He asked to meet the young painter and Manyac introduced them. Picasso and Jacob could communicate only through pantomime since neither spoke the other's language, but they took to each other instinctively. Soon they were meeting every day. With Jacob his constant companion, Picasso learned to speak a French that came to match his Spanish in ease and pungency. Jacob also introduced him to the enjoyment of French literature.

Picasso's earthiness contrasted sharply with Jacob's mysticism, yet his art was beginning to hint at a new introspective spirit. Perhaps he had been spurred by the criticism of Félicien Fagus; perhaps he was simply maturing. In any event, although he continued to paint the café and outdoor scenes favored by the Impressionists, in the fall of 1901 the brightness of his colors gave way to somber tones; realism yielded to sentiment, impersonality to subjectivity. For the first time he displayed a style of his own.

One picture that heralded the change—the most ambitious he had yet attempted—was *Évocation (page 42)*, also known as *The Burial of Casagemas* because it evoked the tragic death of Picasso's friend, who had shot himself in a café some months before. In the painting, the shrouded body of Casagemas is mourned over by cloaked friends. About a dozen figures float wraithlike through a turbid sky. Among them are two groups of nudes, and between them a mother and child. Above them all a woman clutches at the rider of a prancing horse— an image that Picasso perhaps invented to suggest that in death Casagemas was being borne away by the love he could not find in life.

Gone is the light of Impressionism; in its place is an expressive darkness, an all-pervading blue. Gone are the everyday subjects of Impressionism; in their place are ambitious allegories. The only vestige of Picasso's dalliance with cabaret life appears in the nudes floating in the clouds; they are naked except for incongruous, gaudy red and blue stockings—possibly a symbol of their profane love in contrast to the mother's pure love for her child.

The Burial of Casagemas is memorable chiefly because it reveals Picasso's youthful speculations on life, suffering and death, and because it suggests his future artistic course. The mother and child anticipate a series of maternal studies he was soon to do, and the predominance of the color blue presaged his Blue Period.

Picasso provided another foretaste of this now-celebrated phase of his art in a self-portrait that he painted in 1901 *(page 28)*. In it he clearly reveals his own character—that of a strong-willed young man who defies misfortune. But the most striking aspect of this painting is its color, brushed in broad, forceful strokes. It is almost entirely blue. Picasso portrayed himself on a background of deep blue, muffled against the cold in a deeper blue overcoat. Tinged with blue and peering out from the wraps, his mustached face projects a chill isolation.

In the late fall of 1901, Picasso's friendship with Manyac cooled. Unable to sell his paintings elsewhere, he was often close to starving. And as he grew more and more miserable, thoughts of Spain and his family returned. Knowing that he would at least be assured of food and shelter, he left for Barcelona, arriving there in time for the Christmas holidays. Except for a brief trip to Paris in the fall of 1902, he remained in Spain until 1904. There he continued to paint pictures showing lone figures against backgrounds that he increasingly simplified. And in an ever more melancholy mood, he painted almost exclusively in blue.

There has been much speculation as to why Picasso so persistently painted in blue. One easy theory that is often advanced suggests that he was simply too poor to buy a variety of colors. This is hardly plausible, however, for Picasso would sooner have done without food than without paints. Another theory holds that an artist born in Spain, a country of unvarying yellows, ochers and browns, would naturally find monochrome congenial. But this is also improbable, since Picasso did nothing without intent. The simplest explanation may be the best: the color he chose eminently suited his mood and his themes. He was painting the poor of the cities—nameless, hopeless people driven to begging and prostitution and lost in private sorrow. Talking of his sub-

A filthy, squalid beggar probably served as Picasso's inspiration for this watercolor, entitled *The Madman*. Too poor to hire professional models, Picasso used the men —or women—of the streets: paupers and prostitutes were plentiful in the down-and-out sections of Paris and Barcelona where he lived. He was also chronically short of precious art materials and had to paste two pieces of paper together to get a sheet long enough for this sketch. (The line across the figure's knees reveals the seam.) Scrawled at the left is a dedication to Picasso's friend Sebastián Junyer-Vidal.

At 22 Picasso traveled to Paris to settle. He recorded the momentous trip in this series of drawings, a parody on a traditional Spanish picture-narrative form that resembles the comic strip. Picasso shows himself and a Barcelona friend, Sebastián Junyer-Vidal, on the train and arriving in the city, where he is greeted with instant success. The captions below are freely translated.

To the frontier in a third-class carriage.

Arrival at one o'clock: "Wow!"

A stroll through Paris.

Durand-Ruel [a famous art dealer] gives "lots of cash."

jects, Picasso once recalled the poor he had seen as a child in the *chupa y tira* (suck and throw) section of Málaga, so called because its inhabitants ate only a thin soup made with clams they dug at the shore. Their yards were littered with shells tossed from the windows after "they had sucked from them their very souls," as Picasso put it.

Such wretched creatures, many of them blind, all of them alienated from society, became the principals of Picasso's Blue Period paintings. The use of monochrome served to dissociate these figures from time and place; it also served to emphasize that the joys of shifting light and varied color had no place in their bleak milieu. In all the works of the Blue Period, Picasso's intent is perhaps most clearly set forth in *The Old Guitarist*, a study of a mystical El Greco-like figure sitting cross-legged *(page 44)*. There is little sign of life about the man; his shoulders are bony and his pose is cramped, as if to suggest that he finds no ease in the world around him.

In the spring of 1904 Picasso decided to settle in Paris permanently. The reasons for this fateful decision are obscure; one Picasso chronicler has suggested that the artist was finally put off by the "legendary immobility" of his native country. In any event, he set out from Barcelona by third-class coach with a fellow painter, Sebastián Junyer-Vidal. Picasso recorded the adventures of the trip north in a number of sketches he called an "Alleluia," after a popular type of Spanish woodcut arranged, like a comic strip, in a series of scenes. The earliest Alleluias pictured the faithful making their pilgrimage through life; the name "Alleluia" indicated their jubilation on entering heaven.

Parodying these popular images, Picasso depicted the pilgrimage that he and Junyer-Vidal were making to Paris. The final sketch, which shows Junyer-Vidal with a canvas under his arm confronting a frock-coated man with a bag of gold, is captioned, "Duran-Rouel calls him and gives him lots of cash." This was a reference, misspelled, to the influential Parisian art dealer Paul Durand-Ruel, and the triumph hopefully described in the caption must have seemed to Picasso as remote as heavenly reward. Success was, however, imminent.

In Paris, Picasso moved into 13 Rue Ravignan, a dilapidated building on the southwestern slope of Montmartre. Max Jacob christened it the *bateau lavoir* after the laundry boats anchored in the Seine. Picasso lived there for five years, a period he later remembered as the happiest of his life, despite—or because of—the shabbiness of his surroundings. The small room which served him as home and studio had rotting floors and stagnant air. In one corner stood a flimsy cupboard; a makeshift bed was propped against the wall. An iron stove provided a little heat, and an earthenware bowl sufficed as a sink. Canvases, paints, brushes, rags and pots lay in disorder beside Picasso's easel. A pet white mouse lived in a drawer of the table, and a large yellow dog, Frika, was also part of the menage.

Picasso was as poor as the people of his Blue paintings, for sales were few and far between. Vollard continued to buy from him, but irregularly; once, speaking of the late Blue Period, he exclaimed to Max Jacob: "Your friend has gone mad!" When Vollard failed him as a dealer, Picasso had two other choices, each the antithesis of the cultivated Vollard. One was Clovis Sagot, an ex-circus clown who ran a picture business in an abandoned chemist's shop. Sagot, villainous by instinct, openly took advantage of Picasso's impecunious state; in one instance he shaved his offer for a trio of Picasso's works from 700 to 500 to 300 francs. The other dealer was Père Soulier, a former wrestler and drunkard. In his shop Soulier sold bedding, basins and contraband tobacco among a miscellany of art by Renoir, Henri Rousseau and Goya. Kinder of heart than Sagot, he had no idea of the potential value of the works he handled, and once bought 10 drawings from Picasso for 20 francs—about $4.

Poor though he was, Picasso enjoyed his life in Paris. He made dozens of new friends. Three were to change his life: Guillaume Apollinaire, a poet and critic; Gertrude Stein, an American expatriate writer who soon became an enthusiastic partisan of Picasso; and Fernande Olivier, who became his mistress.

Fernande was the daughter of a small-time manufacturer of artificial flowers who had married a sculptor and left him after he went mad. She was young and striking, with auburn hair and green eyes, and she lived at the *bateau lavoir*. One summer day in 1904, as she stood in line with other tenants waiting to draw water from the communal pump in the basement, she became aware of the insistent gaze of her new Spanish neighbor. She thought him not particularly handsome, but liked his piercing black eyes. On a subsequent afternoon she was sitting under a chestnut tree outside the house to escape the heat indoors when it began to rain. Running for cover, she found her path blocked by Picasso, who was standing at the entrance to the *bateau lavoir*, cradling a kitten in his arms. He took Fernande into his studio, and there astonished her both with the white mouse in the table drawer and with the blue pictures that were stacked everywhere.

In time *la belle Fernande*, as she was known, moved in. She fitted into Picasso's life like an odalisque, indolent and voluptuous; he did not even allow her out without him. Her only responsibility was to cook, which was no easy task: Picasso expected her to feed him and his friends on two francs a day. Somehow she managed. For the rest, she listened as the men talked and talked, or watched silently as her man painted. She made no effort to order the chaos of the studio, not even to hang curtains.

For a while their life was tranquil and happy, and the joy Fernande brought Picasso was soon reflected in his work. His whole mood lightened. The somber blues of his paintings yielded to delicate pinks; though the subjects were still faintly melancholic, they were no longer hopelessly outcast. Picasso's new approach was occupied less with compassion than with the customary concerns of composition.

This was the start of his so-called Rose Period. For the better part of six months he devoted himself to portrayals of circus life; harlequins and acrobats supplanted the beggars and prostitutes of the Blue paintings. One of Montmartre's favorite places of entertainment was the Médrano Circus. Picasso loved to watch the show and even more to

Voluptuous Fernande Olivier belonged to the Bohemian circle of artists who occupied 13 Rue Ravignan *(below)* where Picasso took his first Paris studio. The tumbledown tenement building, nicknamed *bateau lavoir* after the laundry barges on the Seine, was home for Fernande and Picasso until 1909.

Picasso once said to his friend Max Jacob, "I have no idea whether I'm a great painter, but I am a great draftsman." These two drawings, made when he was 23, show the clarity and precision of Picasso's line: above is an old circus jester with a small boy; below is a nude youth on horseback. Both were preparatory sketches for paintings.

wander about getting the feel of life backstage. His circus works reflect this dual fascination. Their subjects are clowns in repose and circus mothers tending their young as well as the performing jugglers and bareback riders. Picasso painted them not with the grimly skeletal bodies of the Blue Period but as charmingly wispy figures that seem to vanish into a rarefied atmosphere of light and pale color. Often he depicted them in groups rather than in the solitude of the Blue paintings.

The culmination of the circus paintings is the *Family of Saltimbanques (pages 48-49)*, in which Picasso characterized an entire cast of the itinerant players he had gradually assembled. Like the figures in the Blue pictures, these men and women stand suspended in time and place. But the sense of misery is gone. If the circus folk seem to be gazing inward, it is because they are escaping into a make-believe world where costumes camouflage sorrows. In a sense, perhaps, Picasso was using them to symbolize himself and the isolated role of the artist; but it is clear that he saw these people as he saw himself, without undue pathos.

In the summer of 1905 a new phase of Picasso's Rose Period began in which he retained the pinkness of palette but vastly changed his figures, revealing a fresh concern with three-dimensional form. One of the works of that year, *Boy Leading a Horse (page 51)*, clearly shows this concern; although neither boy nor animal is massive, each has pronounced substance. Perhaps equally important is the fact that both figures are shown advancing, an unusual development considering the static quality of Picasso's earlier works. Manifestly, he was reassessing the old Classical values of balance and proportion. A disciplined objectivity began to replace the allegory and sentiment of the years just past.

Other influences were playing upon him, notably in the person and the poetry of Guillaume Apollinaire. Born Wilhelm de Kostrowitzky, he was the illegitimate son of a strong-minded Polish adventuress who even after he was grown decided the decor of his apartments and kept an eye on his choice of friends. Apollinaire's moon face was incongruously dotted with a tiny Cupid's bow mouth, but out of it issued the most brilliant talk in Paris. There were those who thought him a fraud. But Apollinaire was a born catalyst, and his overweening aim was to sweep out old ideas for new in all the arts.

He and Picasso met by chance in a Paris bar, and soon the studio in the *bateau lavoir* came to be known in Montmartre as the Rendez-vous des Poètes. Through Apollinaire and Max Jacob, Picasso began playing host to numbers of young poets bent on revitalizing contemporary verse. Many sought in their writings to raise subconscious thought to the surface; in this they set the stage for the Surrealist movement that was to sweep all the arts two decades later. Apollinaire's own poetry—which has left its mark on most modern poetry—teemed with original imagery, some of it Classical, some of it exotic, some of it commonplace, all of it lyrical. Convention deterred Apollinaire not one whit. His printed poems appeared without punctuation and set in unorthodox typographical arrangements; a verse about rain dribbled down the page, a verse about love formed the shape of a heart. Picasso ultimately owed a great debt to Apollinaire for publicizing and thus helping to popularize his art; but he was equally benefited by the poet's insistence on total freedom in esthetic expression.

Another Picasso friend—not part of the Rendez-vous coterie, but admired by its members—was Alfred Jarry, a man of macabre humor and antic manner. Jarry's chief claim to fame, indeed notoriety, was a play whose opening obscenities had provoked a near-riot in a Paris theater. Entitled *Ubu Roi*, this opus dealt with a king who embodied all that is base and ignoble in human behavior, yet who was oblivious of his own monstrosity. Jarry served up his hero's nightmarish deeds without passing judgment, without drawing any moral. This detachment, coupled with the fantastic imagery, eventually earned Jarry a place in the pantheon of the Surrealists. Picasso relished his black humor and glorification of horror, and would soon challenge accepted appearances on canvas as boldly as Jarry had challenged them on the stage.

Meanwhile, Picasso's Blue paintings were beginning to find a market. Serious collectors were turning up. One was Wilhelm Uhde, a well-born young German who discovered a Picasso work at Père Soulier's and bought it for 10 francs. A few evenings later Uhde happened into a Montmartre café, the Lapin Agile. Sitting with some artists and poets, he turned to the man on his right and told him about the picture he had bought at Soulier's. The man was Picasso himself. They chatted awhile, then toward the end of the evening, Picasso abruptly pulled a pistol from his pocket—carrying a gun was a prankish habit he had learned from Jarry—and fired a shot into the air. As Uhde recalled it, Picasso was simply expressing joy "at having found a fancier of his art."

But his most important new patrons, personally as well as financially, were Gertrude Stein and her brother Leo. Pennsylvania-born, the Steins had decided that Paris offered a more bracing intellectual climate—a decision made feasible by a small income they enjoyed from their family's investments. They had settled in an apartment near the Luxembourg Gardens. Leo painted and wrote and had an encyclopedic mind, but he was overshadowed by his sister, a short, stocky, masculine woman with darting eyes and a derisive laugh.

The Steins already owned paintings by Matisse, Renoir, Cézanne and Gauguin when Leo, who prowled ceaselessly through art galleries, came upon Picasso's work in Clovis Sagot's shop. Some days later he took his sister to look at the *Girl with a Basket of Flowers*, a blue-toned painting of an adolescent nude; later it would become the focal point around which the Steins arranged and rearranged their ever-expanding collection. As Leo later told the story, Picasso was at Sagot's that day and was so struck by Gertrude's powerful appearance that he said to Sagot: "Ask her if she will pose for me."

Shortly afterward the Steins visited Picasso at the *bateau lavoir* and swept through the studio appraising his work. How many paintings they bought is unrecorded, but then and there they laid out 800 francs —more money than Picasso had ever seen at one time in his life. Picasso's privation was ended once and for all. From then on the Steins brought him a number of other patrons, some of whom Gertrude bullied into buying, whether they wanted to or not.

Alfred Jarry was a Bohemian emulated by Picasso and his friends. An eccentric writer who often referred to himself as "we," Jarry defied every convention, often dangerously. He was fond of carrying a pistol, an affectation that Picasso adopted, and once fired it past the face of a man who had merely asked him for "a light." Jarry died at 34 from tuberculosis that had become aggravated by his habit of sipping ether to get a cheap high.

Picasso's first important collectors, Leo Stein
and his sister Gertrude, were children of a
large, prosperous American Jewish family.
They were well-educated and well-traveled; in
the photograph at the top—taken on a visit
to Vienna—Gertrude, the youngest child, is
at the far left. Leo, two years her senior,
reclines on the floor. Below is a photograph
of Gertrude seated before Picasso's 1906
portrait of her. Not an altogether flattering
likeness, the picture evidently pleased her;
she was fond of saying of it, with the elliptical
terseness for which she was to become
famous, "For me, it is I."

Soon Picasso and the Steins were exchanging frequent visits—at the
Steins' flat on the Rue de Fleurus for Saturday soirées and at Picasso's studio on weekday afternoons for Gertrude's sittings for her portrait. Day after day she traveled across the city to Montmartre, going
part way on a horse-drawn bus and climbing the steep hills to the *bateau lavoir* on foot. While Gertrude posed and Picasso painted, Fernande, who had a beautiful voice, read aloud the fables of La Fontaine.
The usually voluble Gertrude used the time to her own advantage.
Later she revealed that she had "meditated and made sentences" for
a story she was writing.

After about 80 or 90 sittings, Picasso one afternoon suddenly erased
the face on his easel, grumbling that he could no longer "see" Gertrude. He had started the portrait while still in the Classical phase of
the Rose Period; since then his style had begun to change. But the
change had not yet taken definite form, and the new means of expression for which he was groping still eluded him.

By now Picasso's paintings were even more in demand. One day Vollard visited the studio and outdid the Steins' munificence by paying the
unprecedented sum of 2,000 francs for 30 canvases. With the windfall
Picasso took Fernande to Spain for the summer. The portrait of Gertrude Stein lay temporarily abandoned.

Picasso and Fernande vacationed in Gósol, a village in the Pyrenees
accessible only on muleback. There Fernande discovered a new Picasso,
"gay, less wild, more brilliant." Some of the 900 villagers lived by
smuggling tobacco and cattle across the mountains between Spain and
France, and Picasso listened raptly to their tales. He sketched the peasants, he sketched their horses and cows, he sketched Fernande.

The emergent changes in his work took shape. His lines became
heavier, his figures more solid; he tried brown and terra cotta colors.
Perhaps he was inspired by the simplicity of the life around him, perhaps by the color of the countryside. But there was another influence
besides, in a current vogue for primitive and prehistoric art. This trend
had gained impetus from the discovery near Málaga of a cache of pre-
Roman Iberian sculpture and its exhibition at the Louvre a few months
before Picasso's vacation. In Gósol he began to adapt to his painting
the features of this sculpture: severe, regular ovoid faces with narrow
chins; symmetrical noses that came directly out of the eyebrow line;
large, staring eyes; ears that were too high by conventional standards.

One of his most significant works of that summer is the *Woman with
Loaves.* The lessons of Iberian sculpture are evident in the oval shape
of the woman's face and features—repeated in the oval loaves of bread
—and in the subject's immobile expression. No pathos, no emotion of
any sort, mars the tranquillity of line or mood. The woman's serenity
reflects not only Picasso's awakened interest in Classical harmony, but
also his peace of mind among the peasants of Gósol.

When he returned to Paris in the fall, he took up the portrait of Gertrude Stein and painted a new head for it. Because he had moved in a
new direction since laying aside the work, the finished canvas *(page 66)*
is in two quite different styles. The parts he had painted first—the body

with its draped skirt, and the hands—are realistic, but the face is composed in large, flat, severely simple planes characteristic of Iberian sculpture. Yet the eyes are alive and knowing, and the painting captured the essence of Gertrude Stein, in particular her imposing intellectuality.

The Iberian effect of the face was startling, however, and friends at first protested that the portrait was no resemblance. Picasso was undaunted. "Never mind," he said. "She will come to look like that." Gertrude herself was pleased. She cherished the painting all her life.

Soon afterward Picasso painted a self-portrait *(page 52)* in part based on Iberian sculpture. Both in style and mood the contrast with the self-portrait of 1901 *(page 28)* is striking. Whereas the earlier painting shows a Bohemian old for his years and beset by sorrows, the later work shows a young man throbbing with vitality.

More thoroughly stylized than even this portrait is a large painting Picasso executed in the fall of 1906, *Two Nudes (page 68)*, a confrontation of giantesses with faces and limbs rough-hewn as if from tough wood, and painted in the terra cotta Picasso had begun to use in Gósol. But the tranquillity of Gósol had passed. Both figures look as though they were trying to burst out of the confines of the canvas, conveying an uneasiness and tension. The *Two Nudes* is not a pretty picture, but Gertrude Stein once tartly observed: "Every masterpiece has come into the world with a dose of ugliness in it. This ugliness is a sign of the creator's struggle to say something new."

Picasso was indeed struggling to say something new. So, for that matter, were other European artists, and they were searching far afield for ideas. The vogue for the primitive now centered on the art of Africa. Many of Picasso's friends were collecting examples of it; André Salmon, a member of the Rendez-vous des Poètes, owned a fetish, and Matisse some statuettes. The vigor of the African esthetic was proving contagious; a number of paintings exhibited at the Salon d'Automne of 1905 had flaunted an unexampled violence of color and an uninhibited freedom of rhythm and line. A bronze statue in 15th Century Italian style happened to be displayed in the same room with these works, and the critic Louis Vauxcelles, jesting about the juxtaposition, exclaimed: "*Donatello au milieu des fauves!*"—Donatello among the wild beasts!

Into the terminology of art thus came the word "Fauve," applied to the painters of these disturbing pictures—Matisse, André Derain and Maurice de Vlaminck. Although as a style Fauvism lasted only briefly, and artists like Matisse soon dropped it, it left its mark.

Like the disciples of Art Nouveau, the Fauves took the representation of nature as a point of departure and then strayed from it, asserting that their art lay in line, form and color per se. They were chiefly concerned with color: brilliant, opaque and—above all—arbitrary, used for its own sake. Unabashedly the Fauves colored faces green, bodies orange, tree trunks red. More emphatically than any of their predecessors, they declared that art must be more and more independent of nature, free of the inhibitions of literal imitation. Picasso never joined the Fauves, but he shared their liberated spirit. He soon ventured far beyond the point where they left off.

Leo Stein bought his first of many Picassos in 1905, two years after he and his sister settled in Paris. His enthusiasm for the young artist, soon shared by Gertrude, was instrumental in setting Picasso on the path to world fame. Leo was enthusiastic about the works of the Rose Period, when Picasso painted this gouache portrait of him, but he called Cubism an "utter abomination."

The Blue and The Rose

At 9 o'clock on the night of February 17, 1901, in the back room of a Paris wine shop, Picasso's friend Carles Casagemas shot himself in the right temple. The suicide stunned Picasso. Dogged by poverty and failure himself, he sank into a deep despair. Somehow, he continued to work. And, reflecting his mood, he began to paint in melancholic, cold tones, predominantly blue. These pictures—one a memorial to his dead friend—reveal Picasso's compassion for the destitute, the blind and the lame, the outcasts of Paris society whose harsh lot he shared. In painting such moving and evocative pictures as the one shown at the right, he created a unique personal style, his first and perhaps his best known. This was Picasso's Blue Period.

Abruptly, in 1904, Picasso's life changed and his art changed too. He fell deeply in love for the first time, and as his mood brightened he adopted a warmer palette, painting tranquil pictures in delicate roseate tones. Among the most lyrical and captivating of Picasso's paintings, they are loosely grouped as works of his Rose Period. The first of these, paintings of circus performers and their families, radiate a gentle happiness, but later ones contain less and less emotion until finally his work is almost completely empty of sentiment. In the end Picasso concentrated on figures and figures alone, a concern with form that presaged radical changes not only in the style of painting, but also in the course of art itself.

Not a portrait of an individual but a nearly abstract image of loneliness and despair, this painting epitomizes Picasso's Blue Period. It is executed almost entirely in one color—the blue is tinged with cool green—that emphasizes the dejected pose.

The Absinthe Drinker, 1902

Évocation (The Burial of Casagemas), 1901

THE CLEVELAND MUSEUM OF ART, GIFT OF HANNA FUND, 1945

La Vie, 1903

Obvious tragedy and provocative allegory are freely mixed in some of Picasso's Blue Period paintings. The picture at the left commemorated the burial of his friend Casagemas, whose body lies mourned on earth while his spirit, riding a white horse, moves through a sky peopled by lush nudes. More enigmatic is the picture above, which inexplicably contains two small pictures of nudes between the large standing figures. It is apparently about love—mother love, sexual love, platonic love, self-love and perhaps even more specifically about the unhappiness of love. Painted in monochrome, it heralded dozens of such moody, deep-toned pictures.

43

The Old Guitarist, 1903

Having learned how to draw the human figure with astounding precision before he was out of his mid-teens, Picasso distorted it imaginatively during his Blue Period in order to convey the moral and physical decay of his characters. He drew elongated limbs and fingers, painted bony, fleshless bodies, and adopted stylized, sexless profiles—in the paintings above and at right virtually the same head serves for both the man and the woman. Some of these distortions, especially the unusual stretching of hands and arms, were undoubtedly inspired by the paintings of El Greco that Picasso had seen in Madrid and Toledo. And the young artist, with his customary sensitivity, deftly modified the device: the gaunt hand of the blind old beggar plucks listlessly at his guitar; the frail arms of the pitifully thin washerwoman agonizingly transfer her meager weight to the heavy iron.

44

Woman Ironing, 1904

Hands tell an important story in the etching below— a watershed work that stands between Picasso's Blue and Rose Periods. Although the blind man's averted face suggests solitary suffering, his hands warmly embrace his woman. It was while working on this etching that Picasso met Fernande Olivier, who brought not only companionship but beauty into his life. His new-found elation can be sensed in his paintings. He turned to other colors, broadening his narrow blue range to include ocher, warm pink, orange and red. His subject matter changed even more sharply. In Montmartre he met members of the Médrano Circus. Exhilarated by their agility, courage and gay spirit, Picasso painted many pictures of them. Perhaps the most tender is at the right: the acrobat and his family are bound together by an affection that embraces even the pet circus baboon.

The Frugal Repast, 1904

The Family of Acrobats with Ape, 1905

Family of Saltimbanques, 1905

The Jester, 1905

Large pictures seem to represent landmarks in Picasso's work, often summarizing his previous preoccupations in a bold gesture. So it is with the picture at the left. Over 7 feet wide and 7 feet high, it was his first really big canvas and the last Rose Period painting dealing with circus themes. Yet a story is absent in this picture, suggesting a new direction for his art. Here Picasso has assembled, as if for a final curtain call, the characters he had come to know so well: the Jester, old, fat and patriarchal (he also portrayed a young Jester in one of his earliest pieces of sculpture, the bronze bust above); boy acrobats, a young ballerina and Harlequin, the circus actor whose shrewd comments on the action set him apart from the rest. Curiously, Harlequin wears Picasso's profile.

Picasso poses many questions in this summary picture, for although he has dressed his figures in familiar garb, he has left the story that connects them ambiguous. Who is the woman seated at the right, for example? She seems to be a part of the group and yet she is apart from it. Why should Picasso have given Harlequin his own profile? What could this identification signify? All that is certain is that these characters are from the world of the circus. Standing in a featureless setting, they are treated like the objects in a still life, betraying no emotion, no sentiment. The poet Rainer Maria Rilke described the picture as "a tapestry lost in the universe."

49

Lady with a Fan, 1905

Boy with a Pipe, 1905

In the midst of his Rose Period, when Picasso had achieved some artistic recognition and was beginning to gain a little financial reward, he left behind the very styles that had won him success. He was not content to duplicate himself, although he undoubtedly could have made an extremely successful and lucrative career by doing so.

The paintings of 1905 and the following year, three of which are shown here, are among the most innocent and pleasing of all Picasso's works. But despite their popular appeal their precise subject matter can not be defined.

Picasso ruthlessly eliminated specifics from his paintings. In none of these pictures, *Lady with a Fan* in particular, is the viewer told anything about the place the figures inhabit. A sense of time is also absent: no hour, day or season is indicated. Both are irrelevant, for Picasso clearly intended to focus attention only on the figures themselves. Yet these human beings lack an identity; their faces are portrayed without personality or emotion, and Picasso has omitted recognizable costumes such as those in his circus paintings. In the end, the viewer is left to examine the forms, the colors, the shapes on the canvas, and from them to draw his own conclusions and experience his own sensations.

Boy Leading a Horse, 1905-1906

The Invention
of Cubism

Picasso's face is severe and
masklike in this self-portrait,
painted when he was 25. His body
is simplified into crude, bulky
shapes. He had been inspired in part
by the style of pre-Roman sculptures
discovered in Spain and exhibited
in the Louvre, and began to develop
a new vocabulary, adopting some
of the characteristics of this
primitive art in his portrayals of
the human face and figure.

Self-Portrait, 1906

By 1906 the 24-year-old Picasso had achieved a position that any artist
might have envied. A dealer as influential as Vollard was his steady
patron, and collectors clamored for more of his works. His pictures
brought prices sufficient to satisfy Fernande's craving for expensive
perfumes. More rewarding still was his standing among his fellow painters. He was first in his own circle, and his reputation was growing.
Probably no painter was better known in Paris save Henri Matisse.

Picasso met Matisse at Gertrude Stein's one Saturday evening. In later years Picasso found him a good friend, but when they met they had
little to say to each other. Matisse was bearded and self-assured, 12
years Picasso's senior; he looked every inch the master. The violent
colors and arabesques he favored in painting were a far remove from
Picasso's concerns of the moment. Moreover, the two men were vying,
consciously or not, for pre-eminence in artistic Paris, and they eyed
each other like contenders before a championship bout. Thereafter Matisse frequently asked mutual acquaintances: "What is Pablo doing?"

Not even Pablo's closest friends were prepared for what he was doing. No doubt they expected that he would go on mining the rich vein
of the gentle Rose Period paintings. But Picasso has always had too
fertile a mind to be content with repetition. Some time during 1906 he
began work on a painting unlike any he had ever tried—and unlike any
the world of art had ever seen. In all the centuries of Western painting
there have been only a few works that of and by themselves have altered art's future course. Among these is Picasso's study of five female
nudes that was eventually entitled *Les Demoiselles d'Avignon (page
71)*. Often acclaimed as the "first" truly 20th Century painting, it
achieved a basic breakthrough in art, effectively ending the long reign
of the Renaissance. Other artists would learn from the *Demoiselles*
or loathe it, but they would never escape it.

Picasso prepared for the painting as intensively as if for battle. He
made at least 31 preliminary sketches, in charcoal, pencil, pastel, watercolor and oil. He also made sketch upon sketch of the separate figures.
He played with and then rejected the notion of introducing two clothed

males, possibly sailors, into the group of five women *(page 70)*. When at last he turned from preparation to painting, he chose a canvas almost eight feet square—the biggest he had used until then; reinforced it with a backing of other material; had an outsized stretcher made to fit. Picasso seems to have viewed the *Demoiselles* as his magnum opus.

How many months he labored on it is not known. But some time in 1907 he thought it complete enough to show to friends. The reaction was shocked disbelief. Even his most devoted admirers, Max Jacob and Guillaume Apollinaire, found nothing to praise. Leo Stein scoffed: "You've been trying to paint the fourth dimension. How amusing!" Matisse thought the painting a deliberate mockery of the modern movement in art, and vowed he would "sink" Picasso. Desperate for approbation, Picasso sent a message to the German collector Wilhelm Uhde, one of his earliest supporters, begging him to come and have a look. "Somehow he expected a quicker comprehension from me," Uhde recalled later. "Unfortunately, he was disappointed in this hope."

Hardly a person in Paris seems to have grasped the implications of the *Demoiselles*. One exception was, oddly enough, a fledgling dealer —Daniel-Henry Kahnweiler, a German-Jewish youth who had only recently been started in business with a gift of 25,000 francs from his father. He heard about the *Demoiselles* from Uhde and promptly visited Picasso at the *bateau lavoir* to see it. He recognized it at once as a great work. He bought all the preliminary studies and would have purchased the painting itself, but Picasso rolled it up and put it away, as if to hide it from the storm of abuse it provoked.

Today, after 60 more years of tremors and upheavals in art, the shock that swept Picasso's friends on viewing the *Demoiselles* is less easy to understand than in the context of the time. These men were anything but conservative; innovation was their daily fuel. What shook them was the extent of Picasso's daring. As a declaration of independence of existing values, the *Demoiselles* was—even for an era familiar with experiment—an extraordinary manifesto. It did violence to almost every precept of Western painting, recent as well as traditional.

Above all it did violence to the human form. Picasso simply smashed the body to bits—making the canvas remind one critic of a "field of broken glass"—then put the pieces together again in a startling assemblage of angular planes, rounded wedges, facets of every shape. Not content with this heresy, he further defied anatomical principle by discarding ears, placing eyes at different levels, and presenting noses in profile on faces seen from the front; he distorted one figure, the nude at lower right, so that her face and back both show.

Picasso waged psychological as well as physical war in the *Demoiselles*. Had he portrayed only one figure, however fragmented or twisted, he would have jolted the viewer far less. But he chose the more complex theme of a group composition, ignoring conventional perspective and spatial relationships and causing his figures to explode across the surface of the canvas. Moreover, he gave monster heads to two of his five figures. These grotesque masks, marked with frightful slashings, plainly derive from his interest in African art, even as the faces of the other three figures derive from his studies of Iberian sculpture. Whatever Picasso's motive for crowning his conception of the human form with inhuman heads in these two instances, the effect is unarguable: the bizarre intrusion begets a sense of deep tension.

By the use of these ambiguities Picasso struck hard at the longcherished notion that there must be a certain orderliness and propriety in human relationships. Manet had attacked this same concept in 1863 —and kindled similar outrage—by juxtaposing two fully clothed men with a female nude in a contemporary picnic setting in his *Déjeuner sur l'Herbe*. But Manet's painting did not, at least, tamper with the appearance of natural forms, nor did it completely forsake rules of composition and perspective.

Picasso demolished perspective. There is no depth behind his figures; they do not occupy a rational position in rational space. In traditional paintings the viewer has the comfortable feeling of looking through a window into a logically arranged scene, focusing his glance under the artist's careful guidance. The *Demoiselles* offers no such help. Instead, its distortions of face and figure and placement force the viewer to look everywhere at once, sorting out his optical impressions as best he can.

Were this all, the viewer's task would be perplexing enough. But at the same time Picasso is asking him to abandon his preconceived ideas of form, to forget natural appearances altogether, to look at the fragments that make up his nudes as pure forms in themselves.

In producing the *Demoiselles*, Picasso may have found inspiration for one of its features in the paintings of two other masters. The very casualness of his assembled figures reflects something of the spirit of the nudes in a much-acclaimed work of 1906 by Matisse, the *Joy of Life*, and those in an earlier work by Cézanne, the *Bathers (page 70)*. But in the overall concept of the *Demoiselles*, this borrowing—if such it was —was a minor matter, subordinate to the painting's essential message: a revolutionary call for wholly fresh perceptions in art.

Picasso continued to experiment in paint with the *Demoiselles* figures, singly and in groups of two or three, in the same poses and in new ones, to pursue and develop his ideas. He was not a man to be deflected from his course by abuse, but he began to keep his art to himself. Away from his easel, however, he was more gregarious than ever. Every Tuesday evening, protected against the winter cold by an outsized overcoat that dragged at his ankles, he walked with Fernande to the Closerie des Lilas, a Left Bank café where André Salmon and another poet, Paul Fort, held forth at weekly sessions they called "Vers et Prose." The writers in the group read aloud from their current works, and they all told ribald jokes and traded insults, often with a fervor that caused them to be thrown out. On other evenings there were dinner parties in the cellar of Vollard's gallery; the portly Vollard was as attentive to his palate as to his art dealings, and he favored Creole cooking and fine wines. Saturday nights were reserved, as a ritual, for the parties given by the Steins. Often Picasso would stride into the room at the head of a phalanx of much taller cronies; on such occasions, Gertrude later recalled, he reminded her of a bullfighter entering the ring.

When Picasso first spotted this painting by Henri Rousseau in 1908, all that he could see of it was the woman's head looming above some canvases piled in front of it. It was enough to convince him that he was before the work of a master. On seeing the full canvas, Picasso bought it immediately. In the decades that followed, it has remained a favorite in his private collection of work by other artists.

There were also frequent gatherings—more solemn evenings of poetry, songs and monologues—at the home of Henri Rousseau, a small, bent man in his 60s who was called the *Douanier*, or Customs Officer, because he had served in the Paris tax-collecting system. At 41, untutored and unschooled, he had retired to paint. He took this endeavor so seriously that he measured his models with a ruler, transcribed the measurements to scale, then recorded them on canvas. Such earnestness marked his every deed and inevitably made him the butt of many of his friends' practical jokes.

In 1908 Picasso bought a Rousseau portrait at Père Soulier's combination gallery and junk shop. Soulier sold it to him for five francs—about a dollar—telling him solicitously that the canvas was good and he might be able to paint on it. Picasso had no intention of doing so; he later said the picture had taken hold of him "with the force of obsession." Rousseau's paintings were marked by dense foliage and dreamlike figures, yet remained as simple as a child's in their starkness of form. The critics ridiculed the simplicity, but Picasso and his friends found it irresistible. They saw in it a parallel to primitive art, unspoiled by Western dogma.

Georges Braque was as bewildered as the others who viewed it when he first saw *Les Demoiselles d'Avignon*. But that same year he undertook a similarly bold distortion of the human form. *Grand Nu (above)*, influenced by Picasso's innovations, is more importantly an expression of Braque's own lyrical interpretation. In his words: "It is a mistake to imitate what one wants to create."

Another member of Picasso's circle, and soon to be vital to him, was Georges Braque, a fairly recent acquaintance. Braque, the son of a house painter in Le Havre, had come to Paris on a bicycle in 1900 to be apprenticed to another house painter. He had since turned to serious art study, and had exhibited with the Fauves. Unlike most of his fellow painters, he never starved, for his parents sent him a steady allowance; besides, he had the extraordinary luck to sell all six paintings from his first exhibit in 1907. A friend later recalled with envy: "[Braque] always had a beefsteak in his stomach and some money in his pocket."

Braque was among the many who had derided the *Demoiselles*. Yet almost immediately after seeing Picasso's painting, in December 1907, he began work on his own *Grand Nu*, in which he borrowed Picasso's idea of simultaneously showing the nude's face and back. The following summer Braque went to L'Estaque, a picturesque fishing village on the outskirts of Marseilles that had attracted a number of other painters, Cézanne included. Cézanne was uppermost in Braque's mind for another reason as well. Since his death the year before, more of the extraordinary paintings he had produced in his years of seclusion had begun to come to light. His work was being exhibited so frequently that it dominated the talk of artistic Paris; the younger painters were particularly entranced with his geometric reconstructions of landscape. In a deliberate decision to deal with the problems of form posed by Cézanne, Braque turned to landscape. In works like *Houses at L'Estaque (page 87)* he reduced every object he painted to the simplest blocks. Houses were stripped of all detail, even of windows and doorways; treetrunks were simple cylinders; foliage consisted of flat green planes elided with those of houses.

Returning to Paris in the fall, Braque submitted six of these paintings to the Salon d'Automne. They were turned down, and he showed them at Kahnweiler's gallery instead. According to one story Matisse, who was a member of the jury of the Salon, remarked to the critic Louis Vauxcelles that Braque's pictures were full of *petits cubes.* When Vauxcelles reviewed the pictures he wrote scornfully that Braque had reduced "everything—skies, figures and houses—to geometric schemes, to *cubes.*" In the spring, when Braque showed several more paintings at the Salon des Indépendants, Vauxcelles characterized the show as "Cubist." The word took hold.

In one of those fateful coincidences of history in which the same new idea simultaneously crops up in different places, Picasso returned from his summer vacation of 1908 with a number of paintings strikingly similar to Braque's. He had spent his holiday at a hamlet on the Oise, 30 miles north of Paris, and there had tried his hand at landscape. This was unusual for Picasso. Spanish artists seldom concerned themselves with landscape, perhaps because they were discouraged by the monochromatic coloring and the broad sweep of the Spanish countryside. But Picasso, like everyone else, was taking a new look at Cézanne, and that meant taking up landscape. Like Cézanne, Picasso forswore detail and played tricks with perspective. He also distorted the landscape as he had already dislocated the human form. One of his works of that summer, *House in Garden,* merges the surfaces of the roof, the walls of the house, the sky and the trees; it is difficult to tell where the grass ends and the sky begins. While paying homage to Cézanne in this painting, Picasso also bowed to Rousseau: the foliage is jungle-like, and the architecture totally simplified.

Picasso spent the next summer with Fernande in Spain, in Horta de Ebro, the same village to which he had gone with his friend Manuel Pallarés 10 years earlier to recuperate from scarlet fever. One decade had made a decided difference. Picasso had been as poor as the villagers on his previous visit; now he carried 1,000-peseta notes, stirring great local astonishment. He and Fernande stayed at Horta's only inn, the Hostal del Trompet, so called because the innkeeper's son, the town crier, blew a trumpet before making announcements.

I f the austere Spanish countryside did not lend itself to traditional landscape painting, it was made to order for Cubism. Observing the geometric labyrinth formed by the stucco houses on the tiered hills, Picasso produced his first thoroughly Cubist work. In his *Houses on a Hill,* the jagged effects of the *Demoiselles* made way for firm, straight lines, assembled in clustered blocks more pronounced than any composed by Cézanne. Yet the solidity of the houses is offset by a quality of transparency achieved by thin brushwork, so that they seem simultaneously substantial and weightless.

This and other pictures that Picasso painted in Horta inaugurated what was to be the first of several phases of Cubism: so-called Analytical Cubism. The subject to be painted was reduced to its basic parts—pure geometric solids and planes. These parts were then spread on the canvas for analysis—like the components of a chemical compound on a laboratory table—and looked at from several angles and under varying conditions of light. For a time, color was essentially limited to monochrome—first browns or greens, later grays. Picasso may have

A clue to how Picasso arrived at some of his Cubist abstractions may be found in the drawing above, in which a light, realistic sketch of a seated man underlies the dark, cubistic outline. For clarity, Picasso's underdrawing has been redrawn *(below)* to show the figure from which he started.

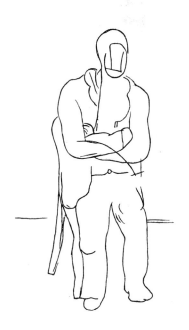

wanted to avoid the distraction of colors in his analysis of form.

Hundreds of miles from Picasso, Braque was spending his summer doing much the same kind of painting. When they met again in Paris in the fall, and through casual shop talk discovered that they were pursuing the same path, they agreed to collaborate. This decision produced one of the most remarkable associations in the annals of art. So intimate and so united in purpose did they become that, recalling the experience long afterward, Braque said they had been like "roped mountaineers." Picasso jokingly referred to Braque as his "wife," and after the collaboration ended, as his "ex-wife." Despite his independent nature, he was no less bound to the relationship than Braque. "Just imagine," he reminisced some 30 years later, "almost every evening I went to Braque's studio or he came to mine. Each of us *had* to see what the other had done during the day. We criticized each other's work. A canvas wasn't finished unless both of us felt it was." Most of these early Cubist works are unsigned on the front; doubts persist to this day as to which of the two men produced certain paintings.

Personally, they made an odd pair; their temperaments were poles apart. "Picasso is Spanish and I am French," Braque said in retrospect. "As everyone knows, that means a lot of differences, but during those years the differences did not count." Braque was as serene as Picasso was volatile, as reasonable as Picasso was capricious, as unassuming as Picasso was flamboyant. Braque, however, had his own idiosyncrasies. For years he wore the typical French laborer's square-toed shoes—but made to order of beautiful leather and kept polished to a high shine. He also sported the workingman's blue cotton shirt, but it was always freshly ironed and modishly accented with a colorful scarf.

He was six feet tall. Well into his old age, according to his neighbors in the village in Normandy to which he had retired, he stood "straight as a cypress." Gertrude Stein, more practical if less poetic, found it "very handy, his being so tall. Without using a stepladder, he could hang pictures on the top row of my studio wall." She might have added that she used the good-natured Braque to hang other men's pictures, for though she once bought two Braques she promptly returned them.

Gertrude's friend Alice Toklas, destined to be her lifelong companion and alter ego, saw Braque in a very special light. To Alice, San Francisco-born, his genial, independent air made him seem so much like an American cowboy that she felt she had to watch her tongue for fear he understood English. Picasso and Apollinaire picked up Alice's characterization and called Braque *notre pard*. This was an expression they had picked up from reading *Les Histoires de Buffalo Bill*, in which "pard" or "pardner" was rendered as *mon pard*.

Although uncommonly handsome, Braque was shy with women. Picasso decided that his friend needed a wife and turned matchmaker. The girl in question was a cousin of Max Jacob, daughter of a cabaret owner in Montmartre. Picasso took Braque and Jacob to rent dress suits, top hats and capes, then led them in making a formal call. The evening got off to a good start, but before it was over suitor, matchmaker and assistant were roaring drunk, and the girl's father threw

This snapshot of Georges Braque was made in his studio in 1910. On the wall are many of the objects he used in his paintings. Of these props, which include the concertina he holds, he later said: "The painter thinks in forms and colors; in the object lie his poetics." Among the extremely limited range of objects that Braque included in his carefully controlled Cubist still lifes, one of those most often seen is the mandolin hanging behind him.

them out. Undaunted, Picasso introduced Braque to another girl, Marcelle Lapré, who promptly became Braque's model. After a few years —in 1912—Braque and Marcelle were married, and lived happily together until his death in 1963.

Picasso and Fernande knew no such enduring joy. Discord seemed to rise in proportion to their prosperity. In the fall of 1909 they moved into a large apartment on the Boulevard de Clichy with a living room, dining room, bedroom and a separate studio with a north light—a far cry from the cramped quarters at the *bateau lavoir*. Their way of life also changed; it was no longer the day-to-day gamble they had loved so well in their earliest days together. There was no more need for them to bed down cozily on winter afternoons to ward off the room's chill; there was no more need for Fernande to pawn her earrings to put together a few francs for food. Picasso took pains to furnish the new place with a purple velvet couch, a walnut dining table and a big brass bedstead; he also decorated it with tapestries, African masks and statues, and guitars. He hired a maid, whom he outfitted with a cap and a white apron, and he and Fernande began to emulate the Steins and other well-to-do friends by giving Sunday afternoon receptions.

Still, Picasso grew disagreeable. He seldom spoke to Fernande any more except to grumble that he was suffering from fatal consumption (actually, he had only a smoker's cough); when she remarked on his silence, he would bark: "I am thinking about my work." Finally he complained that he could not paint in the new studio, and rented another back at the *bateau lavoir*. Fernande, who had stood by him in his years of destitution, now spent her days alone in the pseudo-grandeur of the Boulevard de Clichy apartment.

Despite the personal difficulties of the year that followed Picasso produced a great many works, some of them now landmarks of the Cubist movement. One was a portrait of Vollard, by then no longer Picasso's dealer but still his friend. Vollard's face appears as a profusion of small overlapping and intersecting fragments; the contours have been broken; the lines, instead of fully describing the features they indicate, follow a logic of their own, forming a gridlike structure. Even so, the portrait is a remarkable likeness *(page 90)* in which Vollard's domed forehead, full cheeks and determined mouth emerge distinctly. The subject himself declared that a four-year-old he knew, on seeing the painting, exclaimed: *"C'est Vollard!"*

Soon afterward, Picasso portrayed his faithful collector Wilhelm Uhde. Although the contours are even more broken than in Vollard's portrait, the likeness still faithfully projects an image of Uhde's high forehead, pursed lips and fastidious air. Uhde collected books as well as paintings, and Picasso took note of this in the background of the portrait; inevitably, the books appear as little cubes. Henceforth Picasso habitually surrounded the people he painted with significant oddments of their lives, or accented characteristics which their friends would recognize. As the Cubist style became more cryptic, this technique provided the few clues to the subject's identity.

Braque, meanwhile, was following another tack. During the winter

When he made this photograph of art dealer D.-H. Kahnweiler, Picasso and the gallery owner had been friends for several years. Shortly after their first meeting, Kahnweiler began to exhibit not only the work of Picasso, but also that of Braque, Gris, Léger, Derain and Vlaminck. Always fiercely loyal to his artists, Kahnweiler has said that, "When one supports the work of a painter, one buys all his work. If it comes on the market again, I am prepared to buy it back not to support the price, but because I like it."

of 1909-1910 he painted the *Pitcher and Violin*, in which he broke and distorted the outlines of the violin and other objects, then reassembled the resulting fragments. Whereas Picasso's portrayals of Vollard and Uhde are recognizable, Braque's violin would be scarcely detectable save for the strings, the scroll and the rounded bottom of the instrument. Here was something new: an awakening interest in forms divorced from any identifiable object. But as if to rein in this tendency, Braque added a strong touch of realism to the work: among his strange shapes he painted an ordinary nail, letting it cast a naturalistic shadow over the forms below it.

A subsequent portrait of Kahnweiler by Picasso reflected the move toward abstracting the essence of a subject. Those who knew the sitter well might guess his identity by such clues as the watch chain, the part in the hair, the heavy eyelids and the large ears. But unlike the faces of Vollard and Uhde, the face of Kahnweiler, dispersed in an array of planes, is no longer recognizable *(page 91)*.

While Picasso and Braque experimented, Cubism was gaining adherents. The works of both men were usually on display at Kahnweiler's, and a steady increase in sales reflected a growing acceptance of the new style by collectors. Among artists, one of the earliest converts to Cubism was Juan Gris, who, like Picasso, was an expatriate Spaniard. Five years younger than Picasso, he lived at the *bateau lavoir*, and initially earned a very meager living from the satirical cartoons he produced for newspapers and magazines.

When he turned to painting, Gris made rapid headway. He entered the Cubist movement at once, joining with Picasso and Braque in evolving a new variation known as Synthetic Cubism. The three men replaced the monochrome of Analytical Cubism with bright colors *(pages 96-99)* and also experimented with the use of materials—sand and paper among them—that were hitherto foreign to painted canvases. The aim, as Gris explained it to Kahnweiler years later, was no less than "to create new objects which cannot be compared with any object in reality." Picasso and Braque acknowledged the newcomer's contribution, and used it to their own ends. For a time Gris, who was erudite and rather humorless, insisted on calling Picasso "cher maître," according him the due respect of a disciple for a master. Picasso soon squelched the habit, which he found cloying, but turned it to graceful account after Gris died in 1927. "Disciples see more clearly than masters," he said.

By the spring of 1911 Cubism had taken such hold in artistic circles in Paris that the Salon des Indépendants showed an entire group of paintings that were unanimously labeled "Cubist" by the press. In studios all around the city, painters were examining Cubist theory, exploring it, adapting it. Among them were two young men who were destined to become giants in their own right: Marcel Duchamp, whose brilliant study of a fragmented figure in motion, *Nude Descending a Staircase*, was soon to outrage the public, and the Dutchman Piet Mondrian, who would eventually reduce Cubist geometry to horizontal and vertical lines. The contagion of Cubism spread abroad, encouraging radical movements born of the same zest for total freedom of expression. In Italy Futurism glorified the machine and its motion. In England Vorticism borrowed the Cubist practice of showing several views of a subject simultaneously. Elsewhere artists carried Cubism to one of its logical conclusions: pure abstraction.

If Cubism caught fire in the art world, it was slower to ignite the public —at least in a favorable way. Individual collectors were proudly showing their Braques and Picassos as far afield as New York, Munich and London. But the response of ordinary visitors to Cubist exhibits was likely to be a loud hoot. Reflecting this derision, one Paris critic described a work by the Cubist painter Robert Delaunay as "an Eiffel Tower toppled over, presumably with an eye to destroying the nearby houses, which, dancing a cancan, are rudely sticking their chimney pots into each other's windows."

The cause had its champions as well. André Salmon and other members of the Rendez-vous des Poètes had come round from their early disapproval, and staunchly defended Cubism in magazine and newspaper articles. So did Apollinaire, who took lessons in painting the better to write about it. Eventually several of Apollinaire's articles were published as a book, *Les Peintres Cubistes.* Apparently readers could not resist his flamboyant prose; in any event, he proved to be Cubism's most effective propagandist. Years later Braque confessed: "He never wrote penetratingly about art. I'm afraid we kept encouraging Apollinaire to write about us as we did so that our names would be kept before at least part of the public." Asked to explain how, then, people had eventually come to accept Cubist painting, Braque added: "They never comprehended. They endured. That is the history of modern art."

In the summer of 1911 Picasso, Fernande, Braque and Marcelle Lapré spent a vacation together at Céret, a small town in the Pyrenees. Though it is on the French side of the mountains, Céret was originally part of Catalonia. Its citizens still spoke Catalan and consequently Picasso felt very much at home there.

At Céret both men, of course, busily painted, and it is the works they produced at this time that are the most nearly indistinguishable from one another. Braque's *Man with a Guitar (page 93)* is virtually identical with Picasso's *Accordionist (page 92).* So far had Analytical Cubism come that in the *Accordionist,* for example, only the folds and keys of the instrument and the edge of an armchair are discernible; even the player's head has disappeared. For Picasso, this was to be his farthest foray into abstraction.

Despite the pleasures of collaboration in the sun, he returned to Paris in a restless mood. When he roamed the cafés of Montmartre at night now, he frequently left Fernande at home. Later he was to recall: "Her beauty held me, but I could not stand any of her little ways." One night, after a bitter row, Fernande walked out of his life with 11 francs in her pocket and 40 bottles of perfume in her arms. Picasso soon had a less fiery woman: Marcelle Humbert, mistress of the painter Louis Marcoussis and a friend of Fernande's with whom Picasso had been openly flirting. He called her "Eva," signifying that she was the

Picasso began a new romantic alliance with Marcelle Humbert *(above),* whom he affectionately called Eva, almost immediately after Fernande Olivier left him. Eva's tender charm evidently suited Picasso well, for their relationship lasted for three years, until her death. During that time, he created some of his most inspired paintings.

first woman in his affections. "I love her very much," he told Kahn-weiler, "and I shall write her name in my pictures." So he did, much like a boy carving his sweetheart's initials on a tree trunk.

There was more to this gesture, however, than romantic whim: the idea that letters or words might well serve as an integral part of a painting. Braque had already tried the notion in a work called *The Portuguese*, which he had painted in the spring of 1911. On it he had stenciled the word "BAL" (the French for "dance")—a jarring intrusion of the literal in a work otherwise so undefined. Like the nail that he had painted in his *Pitcher and Violin*, the word was intended to convey a particular meaning; in this case Braque wanted to conjure up a café poster he had seen announcing a local ball.

The lettering in *The Portuguese* had been taken up by other Cubist painters, and now, at the outset of his new love affair, Picasso found an apt use for the device. On one canvas he inscribed "J'AIME EVA," on another "MA JOLIE," a refrain from a currently popular song. With this dual reference Picasso introduced a kind of punning that became standard practice in Cubism. When Gertrude Stein saw the picture she said, "Fernande is certainly not *ma jolie*. I wonder who it is." (A few days later she found out.) Eva's response may have been equally baffled. *Ma Jolie* shows only a seated form, barely detectable. Although Picasso produced several paintings of Eva, as Marcoussis had done, the Cubist style had arrived at a point where no traces of naturalism remained. There is no way to tell from the pictures what Eva looked like.

The use of letters in *Ma Jolie* marked a new turning in Picasso's work. He began to restore other reminders of reality to his painting. Braque, whose youthful apprenticeship as a house painter had taught him how to simulate wood grain, marble and fabrics, was currently using the device of *trompe l'oeil* (literally, "deception of the eye"), so that, for example, a violin, or such fragments of it as he chose to show on his canvas, looked remarkably like real wood. Picasso went Braque one better, adapting a practice that he had learned from his father. As a temporary measure, Don José used to pin paper cutouts on a painting in progress, to try the effects of different combinations of color and form. Picasso also put cutouts on his paintings—and left them there, as integral parts of the work.

One of his most celebrated efforts, *Still Life with Chair Caning*, reflects this new preoccupation. It is a small painting, only 10⅝ by 13¾ inches. The first surprise about it is that its frame is made of ordinary rope. The painting itself shows a wine glass and a slice of lemon, broken into the usual Cubist fragments; the letters "JOU," the start of the word "Journal"; and a *trompe l'oeil* pipestem. These by now were accepted conventions in Picasso's circle. But there was a startling innovation as well. To the canvas Picasso affixed a piece of oil cloth that was a machine-made facsimile of chair caning. Then, compounding the confusion, he painted the cloth, covering it with shadows.

Picasso was not being perverse; he was, rather, posing some tantalizing questions about illusion and reality. The caning on the oil cloth looks as real as though it ought to be rough to the touch; yet it is fake, and smooth. The glass and the lemon look "unreal" because their forms are Cubist; yet because they have been painted, they are "real" aspects of the painting. The rope around the painting is "real" as rope; but because it serves as a frame, it suggests wood carving and therefore functions as illusion.

The excitement of *Still Life with Chair Caning (page 94)*, with its invention of *collage* (pasting), led Picasso to further and more complex juxtapositions of reality and illusion. Braque shared in the new adventure. The two men, with their women, spent the summer of 1912 at Sorgues, just north of Avignon. From Picasso's *collage*, Braque soon came up with the device of *papier collé* (collage, specifically with paper). In *Fruit Dish and Glass*, he pasted wallpaper that simulated wood paneling onto a painting of a still life in a café. Soon scraps of newsprint, calling cards and other bits of paper cut into simple geometric shapes bedecked both painters' canvases.

That summer was, in a sense, a watershed in Picasso's life. A time for change was at hand. In the fall he moved from Montmartre to a new studio in Montparnasse, across the Seine on the Left Bank. Embarking on a new life with Eva, he wanted to change his surroundings. In any event, Montparnasse was replacing Montmartre as the intellectual center of Paris.

Cubism, too, was in ferment. Some of the newcomers to the style—in the belief that they should be able to paint it with full mathematical precision—organized as a group called the "Golden Section," after the term used in the Renaissance to define a certain ideal mathematical proportion. This attempt to codify Cubism did not sit well with its founders. Braque recalled: "They started to lay down the law about how Cubism is like this and not like that and so on. I was hardly a man to start painting Braques in accordance with their rules."

Most of the painters of the Golden Section subsequently abandoned Cubism. Picasso, Braque and Gris continued with the synthetic variety they had evolved. Increasingly they used bright and varied colors instead of monochrome. They put less stress on distortions of form; the objects they painted began to be identifiable again. The reasoned analysis of early Cubism was making room for personal expression.

Other adjustments awaited Picasso. In 1913 his father died, renewing painful memories of their final disagreement. Some months later the "small and perfect" Eva fell ill; possibly she had cancer. By early 1914 war threatened. The world, Picasso remarked, was "becoming very strange and not exactly reassuring."

On August 2, 1914, war came, and most of Picasso's friends scattered. Apollinaire, who was not yet a citizen of France, volunteered for her army and was eventually accepted. Kahnweiler, who was still a German citizen, but unwilling to take sides, fled to neutral Switzerland, leaving behind the valuable contents of his gallery. Braque and the Fauve painter André Derain, who counted himself a Cubist for a while, were vacationing with Picasso at Avignon when they were called up by the army. "I took them to the station at Avignon," Picasso recalled after the war, "and I never found them again."

Revolution on Canvas

Few pictures have caused such a sensation—or exerted such broad influence—among artists as the one from which the detail opposite is taken. *Les Demoiselles d'Avignon* was not to be publicly exhibited for 30 years, yet its quintet of abstracted nudes immediately drew impassioned, hostile reactions from Picasso's patrons and from even the most adventuresome of his fellow artists, who came to his studio to study the figures. The nudes proved shocking not because they were prostitutes—the title was a take-off on a red-light district in Barcelona—but because of the way in which they were painted. Picasso broke every rule in the book: the perspective was flat, the bodies were fragmented into angular planes of color, and the faces seemed like barbaric masks. The painting was a dynamic and revolutionary refutation of all that art had held sacred since the Renaissance.

Picasso did not arrive at this breakthrough overnight. Even in his Blue and Rose Periods, when he had flattened pictorial space and used color for expressive rather than descriptive purposes, he seemed to be moving in this direction. But like all revolutions, this one broke out with a thunderclap. On seeing the picture, the collector Shchukin wept, "What a loss for French art!" In time he and the others were proved wrong. Far from a loss, *Les Demoiselles* proved to be a step forward, the essential step in the evolution of the 20th Century's most important artistic style, Cubism.

Great economy of means characterizes Picasso's technique in this picture: the merest lines define facial features, breasts and arms; flat tones approximating flesh color delineate the sharp planes that create the body's contours. Yet there is nothing flimsy about the figures; they have massive solidity and elemental strength.

Les Demoiselles d'Avignon, 1907, detail

Portrait of Gertrude Stein, 1906

Iberian sculpture, Osuna, Spain, detail

Self-Portrait, 1906, detail

Head of a Woman, 1907

Two strong influences, both largely foreign to sophisticated Western art, propelled Picasso toward the rebellious *Demoiselles*. One was ancient sculpture from his native Spain—powerful figures carved by the Iberians before their conquest by Rome. The other was the art of primitive African tribes. Picasso saw both at large exhibitions in Paris and was immensely impressed with their simplification of forms, accentuated features and great strength. His portrait of his friend Gertrude Stein *(left)* is one of the first pictures in which the Iberian influence is felt. Picasso's assimilation of this style is clear in Gertrude's face, which bears a striking resemblance to

the stone head from ancient Spain above at left. He adapted an exaggerated ovoid shape, flat frontal planes, sharply arched brows and thin lips to suit Gertrude's features. Her body and hands, however, are still modeled to suggest three dimensions in the traditional way.

Picasso went on to create two portraits in the Iberian manner *(above, center and right)*, and then to adapt the even more exotic and unfamiliar stylizations of African tribal art. The bizarre faces below are obviously based on objects like the Itumba ceremonial mask at their left; an almond shape, hollow eyes, wedge nose and heavily striated cheeks betray this kinship.

Wooden mask from East Central Africa

Head, 1906-1907

Mask, 1907-1908

Two Nudes, 1906

13th Century Catalan fresco, detail

Woman in Yellow, 1907

Nude Woman, 1907 or 1908

In the year or so following his portrait of Gertrude Stein, Picasso applied some of the strong stylizations of primitive art to the full figure, creating such monumental giants as the nudes at the left. Here, the evidence of Iberian sculpture is strong: the faces, like Gertrude's, are composed of planes and simplified, the torsos are still bulky and massive.

Following a summer trip to Spain, Picasso also experimented with the style of early Spanish painting, particularly medieval Catalan frescoes *(above, left)*. In his own pictures *(above, center and right)* strong, linear patterns create flat areas that suggest volume, and a few simple zigzags define facial features. From this source and from African sculpture *(below, left)* Picasso arrived at a kind of shorthand, an abbreviated visual language by which he could translate the figure onto canvas in a totally new way. No longer did he play the game of three-dimensional illusion as he had in the torsos of the *Two Nudes*. He stripped forms to basic shapes, chose color dramatically and adapted other conventions of primitive art—slashed ritual markings, for example—to define mass. It all came together in *Les Demoiselles*.

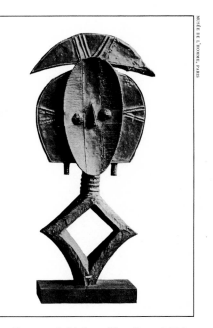

Funerary fetish from West Central Africa

Dancer, 1907

Nude with Drapery, 1907

69

Paul Cézanne: *Bathers*, 1897

Study for *Les Demoiselles d'Avignon*, 1907

I n *Les Demoiselles d'Avignon*, Picasso met head-on what is perhaps the
supreme test of an artist's skill: unifying a large number of figures. Both
challenged and inspired by Cézanne's great *Bathers* series (one of which is
shown at the top above), he made many preliminary studies. At first he
apparently intended to use allegory to unify his group. In his sketch for the
composition *(above)*, a sailor sits amid nudes in a bordello surrounded by
flowers and food; a second sailor enters carrying a skull. But in the final
version *(right)* Picasso eliminated narrative and used style alone to relate
his women. And what women they are! Arrayed like monumental statues on a
shallow, curtained stage, with their bodies fractured into planes of pale color,
they stare brazenly forth from eyes in masklike faces. From the moment
of their birth, painting would never be the same.

Les Demoiselles d'Avignon, 1907

Hommage à Pablo Picasso

Juan Gris

IV

Fame, Success and Marriage

When World War I broke out, Picasso tried to ignore it. He was a Spaniard still, and his native country was not involved. Although sobered by his friends' departure for the battlefronts, he clung to the memory of gaiety. Alone with Eva at Avignon, he painted Cubist pictures that were almost defiantly exuberant, with elaborate patterns and vivid colors. He took cognizance of the war in just one painting, called *Vive la France*, a still life of fruit, flowers, bottles and playing cards all splashed with colors of carnival jollity. Above two crossed French flags appear the words *Vive la*—his gay pictographic salute to his adopted country in its time of peril.

The war was less easy to escape after he returned to Paris in the fall of 1914. Picasso found the city shaken by the German invasion of France and particularly by the terrible battle of the Marne, in which many thousands of men had lost their lives. The front lines lay only 75 miles from Paris, and enemy armies were advancing from the north and east. All France lived in terror that the "Huns" might overrun the City of Light.

Signs of the war were everywhere. One evening, as Picasso strolled along the Boulevard Raspail with Gertrude Stein, a procession of heavy guns rolled past en route to the front. Both the guns and their carriages were camouflaged; bold, irregularly shaped streaks of brown and green paint cleverly concealed the machines of war. The effect was strikingly Cubist, and Picasso was taken aback. "We did that!" he exclaimed.

During the winter Eva's illness worsened, and she had to be moved to a nursing home. For weeks Picasso commuted by metro between her bedside and his apartment in Montparnasse. His loneliness was all the more acute because so many of his friends were away. One of the few who remained was Max Jacob, exempt from service because his health was frail. That winter the ascetic in Jacob won out over the bon vivant, and he decided to have himself baptized a Catholic. He asked Picasso to serve as godfather. Long since detached if not estranged from his religion, Picasso at first made fun of his friend's conversion. He suggested that Jacob take the name "Fiacre" in honor of the patron saint of gar-

In 1912, deeply involved with Cubism, Picasso became the subject of this portrait by Juan Gris. Although younger than Braque and Picasso, the co-founders of Cubism, Gris added his own variations to the style. He reveals these in the rigid, almost mathematical, interlocking of planes and solid forms—cylinders, pyramids, cubes —with which he creates the mass of Picasso's body and face.

Juan Gris: *Portrait of Pablo Picasso*, 1912

deners and taxi drivers (Parisian horse-drawn cabs were called *fiacres*). The jibe was aimed at Jacob's well-known antipathy to women; his proposed namesake, St. Fiacre, an Irish-born hermit, had been a misogynist who refused women admittance to his chapel.

Jacob chose instead to be baptized Cyprien, a saint whose name was one of the many bestowed on Picasso at his own baptism; Jacob was thus paying his godfather a Latin courtesy. At the ceremony Picasso played his role gravely. He gave the new convert a suitable devotional, a copy of *The Imitation of Christ* by Thomas à Kempis, and inscribed it "To my brother Cyprien Max Jacob, in memory of his Baptism, Thursday, 18 February 1915."

This event was one of the few pleasant interludes in an otherwise grim winter. In the prevailing pessimism of Paris, Picasso grew restless, and this mood moved him to take another tack in his art. Much to the dismay of the Cubist painters still at work in the city, he turned to wholly naturalistic drawings. The widespread suspicion that he had betrayed Cubism and gone conservative bothered him not at all. He believed then, and throughout his career, that an occasional change of pace was essential for an artist. "To copy others is necessary," he said, "but to copy oneself is pathetic."

One of his first drawings in this style was a portrait of Vollard, a far cry from his previous depiction of the dealer in Cubist bits and pieces. Picasso described with exquisite precision the contours and the expression of his sitter's face, the wrinkles of his suit, the fold of his tie, the configuration of his hands. That the likeness is excellent is no surprise; Picasso had been a superb draftsman since his boyhood. What is unusual, however, is that he seemed to be consciously imitating the style of Ingres, the brilliant 19th Century Neo-Classicist who was renowned for the clarity and meticulousness of his linear portraits. At the same time the Vollard drawing retained a distinct feeling of Cubism in the projection of the figure against a flat, schematic background.

Jacob, too, sat for Picasso, and Picasso made him look, so Jacob insisted, something like a Catalan peasant. Apollinaire, on leave from the front because of a head wound, also posed. He wore his uniform, the Croix de Guerre he had won for bravery in battle, and an army cap perched jauntily over his bandages. In this portrait Picasso restricted himself to line alone, without shading. Yet Apollinaire's face and posture emerge with near-photographic accuracy.

Picasso's fellow Cubists need not have taken alarm at his foray into naturalism. Along with the drawings he continued to produce Cubist paintings. And he was soon to embark on a venture that would bring him the plaudits of another segment of the avant-garde. Fate intervened to propel him toward this venture, for the opportunity came about as a direct result of the tragic ending of his affair with Eva.

Eva died in the winter of 1915-16. Perhaps hoping to find a place that was free of painful memories, Picasso gave up the Montparnasse apartment he had shared with her and moved to a small house in Montrouge, in a suburb about three miles south of Paris. But the new quarters—even the garden out back—failed to salve his spirit. He made daily trips

Picasso astonished his friends when he began to draw naturalistically after years of painting as a Cubist. Sketches like this one, of his friend Max Jacob, drew cries of heresy from some of the hard-nosed theoretical Cubists, who damned all representational art. More sympathetic critics, however, compared Picasso's elegant and sensitive line with that of the 19th Century master, Ingres.

into the city, sometimes to see Gertrude Stein, Apollinaire and Jacob, sometimes to drop in at the Montparnasse cafés. Usually he stayed so late that by the time he left all means of public transport had shut down and he had to walk the long way home. He liked these nocturnal hikes and the triumphant sense of being up and about while others slept. Occasionally another night owl would join him, and he liked the companionship, too, whether they walked in silent rhythm or talked. One of these new friends, who lived in Arcueil, about three miles beyond Montrouge, was the composer Erik Satie.

Satie was 50, some 15 years Picasso's senior, a man whose personal eccentricities matched the novelty of his music; he regularly burned holes in the corduroy jackets he favored by his blithe habit of stuffing his lighted pipe into a pocket. To sustain himself, Satie had played the piano in a cabaret. When he was 45, his friends Claude Debussy and Maurice Ravel, the leading composers of the day, launched his reputation with concert audiences by playing and conducting his short piano works. A composition by Satie put a performer on his mettle. Just as Apollinaire omitted punctuation from his poetry, Satie dispensed with bar lines and key signatures in his scores. Moreover, he studded his pieces with impish instructions for their rendition; one passage, for example, was to evoke a sound "like a nightingale with a toothache." Further taxing the performer's resources, Satie inserted this directive into a work called *Embryons Desséchés*, which was supposed to portray in music the embryos of three imaginary crustaceans.

Hearing Satie's music was as much an experience as playing it, at least for listeners used to the soothing harmonies of Romantic composers. Satie thought such masters as Wagner and Tchaikovsky pompous and sentimental, and their mellifluous symphonic forms outdated. To him harmonies were less important than patterns of music. He would isolate fragments of melody, many of them reminiscent of American jazz, and repeat them in monotonous rhythms. The effect was at once cerebral and childlike; Satie, in fact, once expressed an eagerness to figure out what kind of music a one-year-old would compose. In his logical yet simplistic approach, his zest for fragmenting and reassembling melodies, Satie evolved a music as Cubist as Picasso's art.

When the two men met, Satie was composing the music for a new production planned by Sergei Diaghilev, the impresario of the celebrated Ballets Russes. The scenario was being written by the poet and budding playwright Jean Cocteau. The 27-year-old Cocteau was prankish and witty, with a gift for brilliant conversation, and Picasso found him as congenial as Satie. The feelings were evidently mutual and Cocteau soon persuaded Picasso to join their collaboration—as the designer of both costumes and sets for the new ballet.

Once again, Picasso's Cubist followers disapproved. For a painter to work for the theater struck them as unseemly. Cocteau later recalled: "A dictatorship weighed on Montmartre and Montparnasse. This was the austere period of Cubism. The objects which could stand on a café table and the Spanish guitar were the only permitted pleasures. To paint a stage set, particularly for the Russian ballet (those young peo-

Guillaume Apollinaire, writer, art critic and Picasso's close friend, sat for several portrait drawings in 1916 while in Paris convalescing from war wounds. This naturalistic likeness honors Apollinaire the soldier, clearly showing the Croix de Guerre medal on his chest and the bandages of his head injury just visible under his garrison cap.

ple had never heard of Stravinsky) was a crime. The Café de la Rotonde was scandalized when Picasso accepted my proposition." Immune as always to the opinions of others, Picasso began to sketch out his preliminary design ideas. In February of 1917 he went off with Cocteau and Satie to Rome, where Diaghilev's company was currently appearing, for rehearsals of the proposed production.

Rome and the ballet were both foreign worlds to Picasso. Each offered its own enchantments. Walking around the city, sometimes by moonlight with dancers from Diaghilev's company, he could admire the sculptural and architectural remains of ancient Rome. The sight of them, and of other antiquities he viewed on excursions to Naples and Pompeii, may ultimately have provided the inspiration for a Neo-Classical phase he was later to enter.

The ballet world was one that he found gaudy and exciting. Along with the dynamic Diaghilev and the dancer-choreographer Leonide Massine, Picasso met the composer Igor Stravinsky, who was in Rome to conduct two ballet productions set to his own revolutionary music. Each man represented in his branch of the arts all the vibrant new impulses of the era. They became fast friends.

The Russian dancers and the ballet orchestra were without peer, and Diaghilev's reputation for staging opulent performances was well established. But he was not one to rest content; he waged constant war against a dry rot of ideas in the settings and scripts of his productions. In the tradition-prone world of ballet, his decision to engage Cocteau, Satie and Picasso—all revolutionaries in their fields and new to the dance—took courage.

The collaborators' venture was *Parade*, a burlesque of a circus that was a spoof unprecedented in ballet. Cocteau took the theme from the dictionary definition of a parade: "A comic act put on at the entrance of a traveling theater to attract a crowd." The ballet depicted the attempts of three barkers to lure an imaginary crowd into a tent by staging samples of their attractions outside it.

A towering Cubistic costume all but overwhelms a male ballet dancer, who is also carrying scenery on his back. This was one of Picasso's curious inventions for the avant-garde ballet *Parade*, whose sets and costumes he designed. Picasso also painted the curtain *(right)*, making it look like a huge circus poster. The first-night audience applauded the curtain, hissed the ballet.

The theme of the circus, familiar to Picasso since his Rose paintings, was natural for him. But in his earlier portrayals of circus life he had painted as an observer; now he found himself a member of the troupe, and an important one. With obvious relish he entered into the whole production; he not only painted the curtain and created the costumes for which he had contracted, but he influenced a basic change in the script as well. Cocteau created the new roles of the three barkers because of some astonishing costumes that Picasso devised.

When *Parade* opened in Paris in May of 1917, it proved to be a disaster. The audience liked Picasso's curtain well enough; it showed harlequins and other circus folk that he resurrected from the Rose Period, although he portrayed them now in greens and reds, and in a distinctly gay mood. The curtain was as lighthearted as a circus poster, and as easy to understand.

But the performance itself seemed incomprehensible. Accompanied by a din of wooden clappers that nearly drowned out Satie's music, two of the barkers stomped onstage decked out in startling Cubist structures —wood-and-papier-mâché boxes that were 10 feet high, hiding all but the legs of the men inside them. The first barker represented a Frenchman; the front of his costume was painted with Cubist motifs and the back with a silhouette of shapes suggesting the trees of the boulevards of Paris. The second barker was an American, as attested by his cowboy boots and skyscraperlike structure. The final barker was actually two men under a shroud—impersonating the front and rear ends of a horse, as in the old circus routine. Four other dancers came on next, in costumes of more conventional fit. They represented the attractions to be seen inside the tents; one was a Chinese magician, played by Massine in a garb of vermilion, yellow, black and white stripes and spirals. In comparison to the barkers in their towering structures, these dancers in properly fitting dress looked like puppets.

The plot of *Parade* was relatively straightforward. Nobody heeds the Frenchman's plea to come inside the tent and see the Chinese conjurer at work. So up steps the American to present an American girl in blazer and white pleated skirt who, in Cocteau's script, "rides a bicycle, quivers like movies, imitates Charlie Chaplin . . . dances a ragtime . . . buys a Kodak." The American has no better luck than the Frenchman. The third barker, the horse, presents two acrobats, who do their stunts. Still no crowd materializes, and the barkers collapse from all their exertion.

Massine's choreography derived its ideas from everyday circus acrobatics. Satie's music, some of it drawn from popular tunes, was as syncopated as jazz. Added to the music were the sound effects of the wooden clappers and the stamping of the dancers' feet. Cocteau also intended to rend the air with the noises of such products of the age as typewriters, a telegraph transmitter, train whistles and sirens, but at the premiere a technical mishap rendered most of these effects unworkable.

When the curtain fell on the prostrate barkers, the enraged audience broke into cries of "*Sales Boches!*" (Filthy Germans!). At any time this was one of the worst insults a Frenchman could hurl; in the climate of wartime it was tantamount to a charge that this affront to esthetics was

Picasso's interest in the grace and beauty of the human figure, quiescent during his Cubist period, was revived by his observations of the dancers of the Russian ballet company. Impressed by their lithe, disciplined bodies, he made many delightful drawings like this pencil-and-crayon sketch, which shows the ballerinas costumed for *Les Sylphides*, one of their most popular successes.

a German-inspired plot to subvert French culture. Cocteau recalled that he, Picasso and Satie, who were seated out front, were nearly assaulted. "The women had their hatpins out and would probably have stabbed us to death if it hadn't been for the presence of Apollinaire, who was in uniform, with a great bandage around his head from his wound." One of the kinder comments they overheard was "If I had known it was going to be like this, I'd have brought the children."

Parade was too subtle, too satirical, too disjointed for conventional tastes of the time. Like Cubist painting, it made use of the modern and the commonplace, and balletomanes accustomed to the romantic and the elegant furiously rejected it. Parts of *Parade* have survived, however. Picasso's curtain and costumes are now museum pieces. Satie's music can still be heard in concert recitals. Massine's choreography provided a fount of ideas for subsequent ballet masters. Another contribution to the future was made by Apollinaire, who wrote the introduction to the program notes. In them he observed that Picasso's designs and Massine's dances represented a new spirit of super-realism, for which he coined the word "sur-réalisme." Within a decade this label was to be affixed to a new art movement that, like *Parade*, fused the real and the unreal.

The ballet produced one unexpected bonus for Picasso: Olga Khokhlova, a member of the corps de ballet. She was not a particularly good dancer, he recalled in later years, but this was no drawback by Diaghilev's peculiar criteria: only half his ballerinas had to dance well—the other half had to be born well. Olga met the second criterion: she was the daughter of a czarist officer. She was also beautiful, ambitious, strong-minded and a stickler for the proprieties. Paradoxically, the normally unorthodox Picasso found a certain appeal in her conformist attitudes; apparently he had forgotten how stifling he had once found his own family's middle-class conventions. Before long Olga had replaced Eva as the woman in his life.

After *Parade* closed, Diaghilev took his company to Madrid and Barcelona. Picasso went along. This was his first trip home in five years. He visited with his widowed mother and his sister, Lola, and old friends greeted him with a round of parties. Between times he turned out a number of drawings. Inevitably, amid the old haunts and familiar associations, they featured bullfight scenes. He also produced some realistic paintings—his first oils in that style since his embrace of Cubism. Among the most striking is a portrait of Olga in a mantilla, showing her fine features and firmness of character.

When the ballet went on to tour Latin America, Olga left the company to return north with Picasso, and moved into his house in Montrouge. This arrangement lasted some eight or ten months. But "Russians marry," as Diaghilev observed, and in July of 1918 Olga and Picasso were wed—in church, despite the bridegroom's less than sturdy beliefs. His good friends Max Jacob, Guillaume Apollinaire and Jean Cocteau served as witnesses at the ceremony.

The couple moved into an apartment on the Rue La Boétie, a fashionable street of apartment houses and art galleries off the Champs Élysées. The place was found for them by Paul Rosenberg, a man of Picasso's age who had become his dealer in Kahnweiler's absence. The apartment stood next door to Rosenberg's gallery. Rosenberg recalls that whenever he was particularly pleased with some picture he had just bought he would rush to his balcony and shout "Pic! Pic! Pic!" Picasso would come running to the bathroom window, lean out and examine Rosenberg's acquisition. Then he would fetch his own latest work from his easel and Rosenberg would appraise it just as informally.

Picasso could afford to live in a plush neighborhood now because, despite the war, he had a sizable income. The failure of *Parade* had only widened his fame, and the market for his pictures flourished. He had as much money to spend as he wished—and Olga spent it freely. She decorated the apartment lavishly and in the latest fashion, with a living room all in white and a bedroom sporting a new fad, twin beds. Floor-length draperies hung at the windows and handsomely framed pictures hung on the walls: Cézannes, Renoirs, Corots and some of Picasso's Cubist paintings. Picasso rented a similar apartment on the floor above to use as a studio. There he kept to his Bohemian habits and usual clutter. But otherwise, under Olga's influence, he became notably bourgeois. He took to wearing tailored suits, with a gold watch chain attached to his buttonhole. He groomed his hair meticulously and tucked a handkerchief into his breast pocket. He also uncomplainingly walked his wife's Russian wolfhounds.

In just a few months Picasso's happiness was marred by the death of Apollinaire. The staunch champion of Cubism, still weak from the head wound sustained in battle, fell victim to influenza. All through the day of November 9 he lay in a coma. In the streets below his window crowds were chanting, "*À bas Guillaume!*" From the spasms crossing his face, Olga, who was at his bedside with Picasso, wondered if he thought the cries of "Down with Guillaume," directed at Kaiser Wilhelm of Germany, were meant for him. She and Picasso sat with him for several hours, then walked home in the evening. As they went through the arcades of the Rue de Rivoli a swirl of air blew the veil of a passing widow across Picasso's face, an omen that chilled him. Before the night was over the telephone rang, bringing the news that Apollinaire was dead. Two days later the Armistice was signed. World War I ended and with it an era closed.

Picasso's association with the ballet and his marriage to Olga had already altered his way of life. Apollinaire's death augured further change; it deprived Picasso of one of his most cherished friendships. His old circle was breaking up. Jacob was soon to enter a monastery, becoming a lay brother at the Abbey of Saint-Benoît. Braque had returned from the war with a head wound and temporary blindness, and he was understandably irritable. He scorned Picasso's dalliance with the theater and *Le High-Life*, as the French call it. Although the two founding fathers of Cubism were civil to each other, they were never again to be close.

In 1919 Picasso had a second invitation to accompany the Ballets Russes, this time for a production to be introduced in London; thus he finally reached that city nearly 20 years after first setting out for it.

Stimulated by the ballet circle that he entered in 1917, Picasso happily drew portraits of his new acquaintances. Shown above are the mustached Sergei Diaghilev, the Russian ballet's impresario, and Alfred Seligsberg, a lawyer for millionaire Otto Kahn, the American patron of the company. Below is the composer, Erik Satie. Picasso designed costumes and sets for four of Diaghilev's ballets—and married one of the ballerinas, Olga Khokhlova.

Diaghilev was staging *The Three-Cornered Hat*, a 19th Century Spanish novel of a local grandee's attempted seduction of a village girl. The story had already been set to music by Picasso's countryman, the composer Manuel de Falla. Picasso's designs for it had none of the drastic innovations of *Parade;* instead, he aimed at an evocation of his native land. His curtain featured a bullfight; a backdrop was painted chiefly in ocher and pink. His costumes for the villagers drew on the rhythmic decorative patterns of the traditional Spanish peasant wagons. On opening night he stood in the wings, touching up the dancers' costumes just before they went onstage. The choreography was as authentic as the music and the designs, for Massine modeled it on Spanish folk dances, the *jota,* the *farruca* and the *fandango.*

The Three-Cornered Hat was as sensational a hit as *Parade* had been a failure. The English loved it. Picasso, Olga, Diaghilev, Massine and de Falla were wined and dined all over London. Picasso took time, however, to make some exquisite line drawings—again in the style of Ingres—of his ballet friends, including a portrait of de Falla, and a double portrait of Diaghilev and Alfred Seligsberg, a lawyer.

Picasso's remarkable ability to create natural likenesses is nowhere more evident than in this meticulous portrait of his son Paulo on a donkey. It was based on the photograph above, but the plump boy, a favorite subject for his doting father, often sat as a live model as well *(slipcase).*

Buoyed by the London venture, rejoicing in a world at last at peace, Picasso was ripe for an entire series of explorations in art. Back in Paris, he pursued whatever style his whim dictated. He painted his old love, the clown, and his new love, the dancer. He also painted bathers by the sea and peasants in the countryside where he and Olga summered. But he painted them in a variety of ways: with the unerring realism of his recent portrait drawings, or with a mannerism reminiscent of certain 16th Century Italians, elongating their figures and attenuating their limbs. By 1920 his work was showing the fruits of his watchful rambles amid the ruins of ancient Rome three years before. A pronounced Neo-Classicism emerged in many of his paintings, studies of tranquil figures such as the *Seated Woman (page 113),* earthy rather than delicate, and massively conceived.

Nor had Picasso forsaken Cubism. In 1921 his Cubist style reached its apogee with two large paintings identically called *Three Musicians (pages 100-101).* Both are over six feet square, and in the full bloom of his vigor he produced them over the period of the summer, working on both pictures simultaneously.

Both works show a Pierrot, a harlequin and a monk, all masked, all sitting stiffly in a row. Both paintings are at the same time simple and complex. They have the flat, playing-card quality of Synthetic Cubism, but at the same time a sense of depth, achieved by Picasso's skillful juxtaposition of planes—brilliantly colored, in blue, red, yellow and white. The familiar Cubist fragments all fit together as precisely as in a jigsaw puzzle. Not one piece is superfluous; each is indispensable to the design.

Vestiges of Cubism were to remain ever after in Picasso's work, but the movement as a whole was in decline. A special sort of death knell sounded for it in a calamity that befell Picasso's friend and dealer Kahnweiler, the early champion of *Les Demoiselles d'Avignon.* When the German-born Kahnweiler took haven in Switzerland at the start of

the war in 1914, the French government seized his gallery as the property of an enemy alien and put the contents in storage. Kahnweiler returned to Paris after the war, not to reclaim his property but to build his business anew. Although he had remained aloof from any involvement in the war and might have merited some consideration on this score, the government in 1921 decided to dispose of his paintings by selling them at public auction.

The contents of Kahnweiler's old gallery consisted of some thousand paintings that would command about $100,000,000 today. Even then they were worth a fortune, for they represented virtually all of the output of the major Cubists; Kahnweiler had been their principal patron. Kahnweiler protested the sale not only in his own behalf, but in the interests of the Cubists and indeed of the government. He pointed out that the release of so many works would glut the market, drive prices down, and deprive the artists of a good deal of money. Oblivious to the potential value of the treasure in their hands, the government bureaucrats stubbornly held to their decision to sell the entire cache in four lots over a two-year period.

On the day before the sale of the first lot, the paintings went on display. In a show of moral support, many important collectors, patrons and artists turned up, whether or not they had a personal stake in Cubism or a connection with Kahnweiler. The affair turned into a Donnybrook. Alice Toklas attended with Gertrude Stein and later reported the particular reaction of the great Matisse. Although neither a Cubist nor a Kahnweiler client, Matisse blistered the art expert who was the government's deputy for the occasion, shouting that the "artistic patrimony of France" was being "robbed." Braque, who had a number of paintings about to go on the block, joined physically in the fray, punching the government's man in the nose—and got himself carted off to the police station by the gendarmes.

The atmosphere at the sale the next day was grim. Kahnweiler dolefully bought up what he could, but that was very little, as the confiscation had left him without any money to speak of. Generally, the paintings went at rock-bottom prices, as Kahnweiler had predicted. Collectors from England and America bought in wholesale lots. Many of the Cubist paintings on view today in the museums of those countries were acquired in that sale and the three that followed.

In February of 1921, Picasso and Olga had a son, whom they nicknamed Paulo. With all children Picasso is tender. His own first born delighted him; he played with him often, and inevitably the child became a favorite subject to paint and draw. Sometimes Picasso showed his son feeding, sometimes playing in his mother's arms, and, when Paulo grew bigger, dressed as a harlequin *(slipcase)*. The serenity of these pictures offers an interesting contrast to the wistful solitude of the maternal scenes of the Blue and Rose Periods.

In the world of art beyond Picasso's door unrest was rife. Disillusionment in the wake of war swept the artistic community as it did all other sectors of the population. Nihilism, a denial of all established values, seemed the only answer. What good was a society that had spawned the anguish, the mass murder, the senseless destruction of war? What good was its art?

The artists' initial salvo against society took the form of a movement called Dada, itself a nonsense word devised to mock the absurdities of a world gone mad. The Dadaists had not awaited the end of war to proclaim their abhorrence of it. They had launched their movement in a café in neutral Zurich in 1916, soon after the holocaust of the battle of Verdun. Poets and painters dressed in crazily daubed cardboard cutout costumes would shout nonsense verse in unison against a cacophony of pseudo-jazz. Soon such assaults on artistic tradition were repeated throughout Europe. Young poets composed by pulling words out of a hat and assembling them willy-nilly. Young painters, with or without paint, produced clutters of unrelated objects.

Otherwise preoccupied, Picasso played no part in the paroxysms of Dada. The Dadaists honored him nonetheless. Picasso paintings hung on the walls of the Zurich café, and a reproduction of one of his drawings appeared in the first issue of the inevitable journal the Dadaists published. But essentially Dada was against all art, and in this negativism lay the seeds of its demise: in deriding the old forms of art it offered no substitutes. Its major legacy was an invitation to see art, like life, in terms not of immutable laws but of constant and unpredictable change. Henceforth all young rebels who wrote verse that did not scan, who painted on plastic rather than on canvas, owed a debt to Dada.

Dada's successor movement, Surrealism, was, like Dada, first articulated by poets. But unlike the Dadaists the Surrealists offered alternatives to the traditions they disdained. In art they proposed to add a whole new set of terms to the existing vocabulary, stimulated by Freudian probes of man's secret mind.

The way was paved by André Breton, a young poet and friend of Picasso's, and author of the *Surrealist Manifesto*. With a few fellow

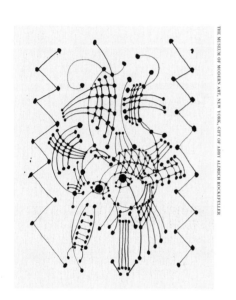

Doodle-like designs, composed of dots and lines, appeared briefly in Picasso's work in the mid '20s. Imaginative networks such as the one above sometimes hint at figures or musical instruments but are most often pure abstractions. In them, as in the ink blots used for psychological testing, the viewer must find his own subject. Picasso filled 40 pages of a sketchbook with these enigmatic ink drawings. No two are alike.

poets, Breton conducted a series of experiments in "automatic" writing. Breton and company would take pen in hand, try to banish all conscious thoughts, and let the unconscious flow onto the paper in the form of words, sentences, and images of every kind. The value of the result, they argued, was that it was a pure expression of an inner state.

They also explored the world of dreams and fantasy. They were particularly attracted by the paintings of Hieronymus Bosch, including his *Temptation of St. Anthony* and his *Garden of Delights.* In these works, Surrealist artists insisted, Bosch had painted in 16th Century religious terms the same moral nightmares that needed to be laid bare in the 20th. More recent inspiration came from the works of Odilon Redon, the 19th Century French Symbolist who had painted strange worlds in which massive Cyclops' heads floated above the sea and winged centaurs shot arrows at the sun.

Picasso admired Breton and much of his philosophy. He shared the Surrealists' conviction that large sources of subject matter waited to be tapped in art. But Surrealism offered little that was new in the way of a formal pictorial style, and Picasso never became a full-fledged member of the movement.

In a sense, however, he became its mentor. In July of 1925 the magazine *La Révolution Surréaliste,* which Breton edited, reproduced several of Picasso's works, along with a glowing critique. Among these works was *Les Demoiselles d'Avignon,* reproduced for the first time since Picasso painted it 18 years before. In the same issue Breton reproduced a brand-new Picasso painting, *The Three Dancers (page 119),* and used it to illustrate a fundamental Surrealist tenet that "beauty must be convulsive or cease to be."

Yet the painting represented far more than a salute to Surrealist doctrine: it was the harbinger of a new style in Picasso's art, unleashing his inventive powers as never before. Picasso did not altogether overthrow his former guidelines. Difficult though it may seem on first glance to detect, an element of Classicism remains in the arrangement of the dancers: the theme of dancing figures in semicircular array goes back as far as the vases of ancient Attica. Moreover, Picasso retained a feature of his earlier Cubist days in an imitation of collage. In the dancer on the left, fragments of the body look as though they were made of swatches of patterned fabric and cut with a pinking shears; actually, they are painted. What is new, however, is the nature of Picasso's attack upon the human form. The attack he had perpetrated in the *Demoiselles* was savage. But by comparison with the figures in *The Three Dancers* the nudes in the *Demoiselles* seem models of academic decorum.

No longer is Picasso content merely to dislodge an ear or up-end an eye or shatter an arm. This time breasts become eyes, limbs are unrelated and torturously stretched or twisted, substance and shadow are interchangeable. Any resemblance to known anatomy seems purely coincidental. Picasso's *Dancers* are not human; they are, at best, humanoid. Of the three figures, the most extraordinary is the one at the left. What passes for a head appears to be in double profile, with two noses. One nose is upturned, the other extends downward like an elephant's

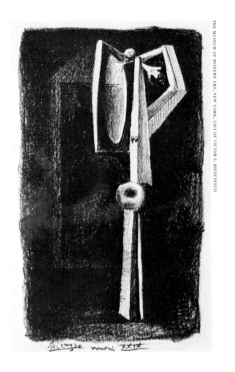

Picasso's continuing experimentation with the human figure, in even more daring forms than he had created during his Cubist period, led in 1929 to this startling lithograph. One of a series of imaginative forms based on bathers at the seashore, it pictures a woman with a ball-like head and arms like steel girders, stretching in the sun outside her cabana.

trunk, seeming to function also as an arm. What appears to be an eye lies between the noses, over another feature that may be a mouth, a breast or another eye. The grotesque mask that Picasso had set upon the nude at the extreme right in the *Demoiselles* is at least identifiable as a mask. His dancer, however, is a sheer monster, a herald of many that would populate Picasso's canvases in the years ahead.

The Three Dancers offered a field day for the young sages of Surrealism. Its double images could be interpreted as an expression of the Freudian concern with split personality. Its contempt for conventional form could be hailed as a deft jibe at the frailties and failures of conventional society. Picasso may or may not have intended to convey these messages. But artistically the work is as historic a statement as the *Demoiselles*. In even stronger terms it proclaims that the artist need not imitate natural forms; he can, and indeed he should, create his own. *The Three Dancers* aptly summed up Picasso's conviction that "nature and art are two different things. Through art we express our conception of what nature is not."

As the 1920s wore on, Picasso intensified his interest in the total metamorphosis of the human form. Paintings and drawings came from his hand without stint. He was nearing 50, and could well have rested on his oars. He had none of the economic pressures to produce that had marked the lean years at the *bateau lavoir*. Life with Olga and Paulo lacked little in material comfort. With his wife in chic attire at his side, Picasso was a familiar figure at first nights and at the fancy balls of the smart set. Summers away from Paris were spent at playgrounds of the idle rich: 1927 at Cannes on the Riviera, the next two summers at the fashionable bathing resort of Dinard in Brittany. There the Picassos occupied a large villa built in Art Nouveau style, and Paulo had an English governess.

For all these pleasures, Picasso's output was unremitting. Frequent escape into the solitude of creativity was as essential as a fresh intake of air, and as bracing. His work continued to bespeak enormous vigor and versatility. Having embarked upon a quest for metamorphic forms, he followed it down a dozen different avenues.

His observations on the beach at Cannes produced a series of charcoal drawings of giant figures like strange rock formations; yet they have a look of life, as if they were primordial creatures oozed out of the sea. Despite their huge size and their total lack of recognizable features, Picasso endows them with a certain droll charm; playfully he shows them as bathers on a beach—one turns the key in her cabaña door.

Different metamorphic types subsequently emerged in pen-and-ink drawings and in oils. One version had a peglike head and arms and legs like paddles, imparting a distinct impression of mobility. Another was more static, a purely geometric construction with a triangle or a pointed oval for a head, rectangles and circles for torso, and stick-straight lines for limbs. Picasso also created a new kind of monster—a chilling amalgam of human bones and vises and various other instruments; the paintings of this series belong to his so-called Bone Period.

Of all the forms that flowed from his fertile mind during this period,

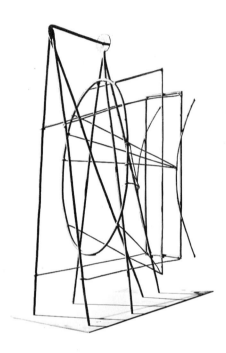

Looking like a radar antenna, this geometric sculpture was actually a model for a giant construction based loosely on the human form. Picasso made it from iron wire in the late '20s, one of several ideas he suggested as a monument to Guillaume Apollinaire. Unfortunately, the group of Apollinaire's friends who were financing the project found all of Picasso's ideas unsuitable, and the memorial was never completed.

one of the most baffling appeared in a painting called *Woman in an Arm-chair (page 120)*. A semblance of a human head inclines atop a semblance of a torso with dislocated breasts. But what mystifies most about this curious blob is its profusion of overlapping limbs, instantly remindful of the tentacles of an octopus. Which of these limbs are arms, which are legs, and which indeed are the legs of the chair in the painting's title—all this remains Picasso's secret.

Predictably, Picasso's newest exploration of form led him into the field of sculpture. He was by no means untried in this art. More than 20 years earlier, while in the Classical phase of the Rose Period, he had fashioned the head of Fernande Olivier, the head of a jester with pointed cap, a young female nude and a toreador's mask. Modeled in plaster —Vollard later had them cast in bronze—these studies in three-dimensions were naturalistic and so effectively executed that for a time Picasso may have considered concentrating on sculpture. He tried his hand at it again during the first flush of the Cubist style. One of his sculptures of that time was a bronze *Woman's Head (page 90)*, in which the surfaces are sharply broken into facets.

But after two decades, and with the emergence of his metamorphic forms, Picasso saw a new kind of challenge to his inventiveness in sculpture. He began by translating into three dimensions the images of the romping metamorphic giants he had sketched in charcoal at Cannes; he modeled them in clay or plaster and later had them cast in bronze. Then for a while he rejected traditional methods and materials. He began to work with iron: rods, from which he made diagrammatic constructions much like outsize three-dimensional doodles; and sheet metal, which he turned into abstract human heads and guitars, sometimes embellished with Cubist designs in black and white paint. .

As the projects grew more complex, Picasso drew on the help of an old Spanish friend living in Paris, Julio González, a sculptor who was also a master metalsmith. Under the guidance of González he produced a number of abstract pieces in which bars and sheets of iron were welded together. In other pieces that would inspire the practitioners of Pop Art three decades later, Picasso jovially assembled iron scraps—springs, pot lids, sieves, bolts, screws, pokers—much as he had put together unexpected pieces of newspaper and rope in his collage paintings. "I find myself once more as happy as I was in 1908," he remarked to González.

Picasso made this comment some time during 1931. If he was happy at his work, he was less so in his private life. That year he bought a small 17th Century château, with gray stone walls and a slate roof, set in a wooded area near Boisgeloup, a village northwest of Paris. The château was handsomely appointed, and across its courtyard stood a row of stables that Picasso converted into studios.

Despite his new role as a man of property, Picasso was assailed by a sense of impermanence. Marriage to Olga was beginning to pall. Beyond Boisgeloup, the world was heading for disaster. Friends recall that even when he was at the work he loved, Picasso seemed possessed by some great inner rage. Before long he would channel that rage onto canvas; in the meantime, he was to find respite in a new inspiration.

Art in the round could well describe Picasso's work in the early '30s when he produced pictures and sculpture like those above and below so full of swirls and billowing lines that he seemed to translate everything into curves. During that period he was in fact concentrating his attention on the curves of the human face and figure and exaggerating their natural aspects. In so doing, he retained the essence of the forms, yet presented them in a distinctive way.

A World in Little Cubes

When the revolution foreshadowed by Picasso's painting, *Les Demoiselles d'Avignon*, broke out in full force in 1908, Picasso was joined at the forefront by Georges Braque. Although Braque at first was shocked by the daring picture, it had evidently made a deep impression on him. In the fall of that year, when the two men returned from their separate summer working trips, they met and compared their works. And they were startled to find them extraordinarily similar. They had simultaneously invented a new style of painting—Cubism.

Cubism grappled with the age-old problem of how to reduce the three-dimensional natural world to an irrevocably two-dimensional canvas. Picasso's and Braque's early Cubist paintings, such as the one at right, showed forms essentially as simple, geometric solids. Gradually they began to slice nature into paper-thin planes, each with one aspect of reality embossed on it, like a name on a calling card, and to spread those planes out on the canvas so that cumulatively they would add up to the desired result. They also limited their color almost exclusively to browns, grays and greens, believing that the essence of painting was form.

Armed with this analytical rationale, Picasso and Braque began a unique five-year collaboration. In time, they were joined by other adventurous artists, most notably Picasso's fellow-Spaniard Juan Gris. This fraternity became the influential Cubist movement.

Reduced to the elemental forms of geometry, this landscape and the few others exhibited with it, inspired the noted French critic Louis Vauxcelles to deride them as composed of nothing but *"cubes."* Even Matisse found only *"petits cubes."* The name, although simplistic, became a catchword.

Georges Braque: *Houses at L'Estaque*, 1908

Like a family tree, these three pictures can be used to trace the evolution of Cubism. At the left, below, is a still life by the 18th Century master Chardin. It is a meticulous illusion, in which the objects are lovingly rendered to appear as if seen through a window. Beside it is a still life by Cézanne, painted more than a century later. Cézanne has taken liberties with nature, trying to show the viewer more than he could see through a window. He has tipped the plane of the table forward to reveal objects that would normally be concealed by those in the foreground and painted things not so much to imitate them but to reveal their essences. At the right is an early Cubist still life by Picasso. He has taken Cézanne's ideas a step farther —representing objects with a stricter eye to their basic forms and tilting the table even closer to the surface of the canvas in order to force the viewer to recognize that his art is limited to two dimensions.

J.B.S. Chardin: *Still Life: The Kitchen Table*, c. 1728-1730

Paul Cézanne: *Still Life: Jug of Milk and Fruit*, 1888-1890

Fruit Dish, 1908-1909

Woman's Head, 1909

Once the Cubist style had been defined, everything became grist for its mill—landscape, still life and portraiture. Picasso's friends became the willing victims of his geometrical dissections when they sat for him. Fernande Olivier, his mistress and therefore his most available model, saw her face reduced to sharp-edged planes in one of the earliest pieces of Cubist sculpture *(left)*. When Fernande was translated to two-dimensions on canvas *(below, left)* all the details of her face were presented simultaneously, creating an unflattering, but uniquely revealing composite image.

Cubist portraiture never totally obliterated the personalities of its subjects. Indeed, Picasso's portraits of the prominent Paris art dealers Ambroise Vollard *(below, right)* and Daniel-Henry Kahnweiler *(right)* preserve their subjects' identities with remarkable precision. Vollard's domed head, protruding jaw and ruddy complexion—the only touch of warm color in an otherwise muted picture —combine with a forceful mien to transmit a strong feeling of his character. Kahnweiler can be identified in his rather more abstract portrait by the loops of his watch chain, aquiline nose and carefully parted hair.

Portrait of Fernande, 1909

Portrait of Ambroise Vollard, 1909-1910

B y 1911, Picasso and Braque had worked so closely together that their pictures, two of which are shown on these pages, are almost impossible to tell apart. Even the artists themselves had some difficulty in identifying several of them later. Picasso has described his relationship with Braque as a kind of marriage. They were in each other's studios daily, trading ideas and discussing techniques. For a few years they even vacationed together. And although here Picasso's work *(above)* is signed, the two men also periodically stopped signing their names on the fronts of

THE SOLOMON R. GUGGENHEIM MUSEUM COLLECTION, NEW YORK

Accordionist, 1911

Georges Braque: *Man with a Guitar*, 1911

their canvases during this period, as evidence of their complete and selfless dedication to a common goal.

At about this time their work also became increasingly abstract, so that it was often almost impossible to discern the subjects. Both paintings shown here, for example, are of seated musicians, but the only identifying clues are subtle—a few cleflike scrolls suggesting the arms of chairs in both pictures, a row of parallel lines like guitar frets at the right center of Braque's picture, and a few accordion pleats in the same area on Picasso's.

Only four years after its birth, Cubism threatened to become a sterile exercise. Picasso and Braque had taken it to the point of almost complete abstraction in 1911, but then they retrenched and began to introduce more obvious reminders of the real world into their paintings. This first took the form of words or letters. In the picture above, the letters "JOU" are part of *Le Journal*, a French newspaper. Here, Picasso also invented a new technique called "collage" by pasting on his canvas a piece of oil cloth printed to look like chair caning. To pose the question of what is "real" in the picture and what is not, he painted shadows across the fake chair caning, adding a painter's illusion to a commercial illusion. And in order still further to enforce this question, he framed his painting with rope, imitating the common decorative wood and plaster gilded frame.

Still Life with Chair Caning, 1912

Georges Braque: *Musical Forms (with the words Fête and Journ)*, 1913

Braque and Gris also contributed to this interplay of illusion and reality by adding words to their canvases *(right)*, by imitating the textures of wood and fabrics, and by pasting real scraps of paper, principally newspaper and wallpaper, to their partly painted pictures. At the right, below, Gris made a pun on the whole technique by pasting onto his canvas a newspaper headline "LE VRAI ET LE FAUX" (The True and the False).

Juan Gris: *Still Life: The Table*, 1914

Portrait of a Young Girl, 1914

With the invention of collage and *papier collé* (the technique of pasting scraps of paper onto a canvas), Cubism took an important step that gave it new life. If Picasso, Braque and Gris had insisted upon painting basically monochromatic dissections of form, they probably would have reached a dead end even with the addition of the pasting processes. The visual jokes and puns of those techniques could only have had a limited application in formal painting. But in the next few years they began to add color to their paintings again and in a joyous burst of relief they reintroduced textures as well. Picasso's brilliantly decorative *Portrait of a Young Girl (left)* positively exults in a profusion of illusionary textures—some dozen different commercial printed papers are imitated—subtle colors and suggestive shapes. The outline of the girl's body resembles that most familiar Cubist object—the guitar. In Braque's still life *(below)*, he shows a dislocated guitar and other objects with a sure command of form and in bold patterns of dense colors that reveal his sober, balanced hand. In the years to come, Braque would continue to mine the resources of Cubist still life with great skill. Still life also preoccupied Gris, as his picture on the following pages will testify. There, in a wonderful interplay of space and illusion, Gris shows a book and a guitar lying on a table in front of a shuttered window through which a snow-capped mountain range can be seen. But Gris has brought the outside in by mirroring the contours of the range in the bottom edge of the guitar and duplicating the peak of the mountain in the upper angle of the table.

Georges Braque: *The Black Pedestal Table (Le Guéridon Noir)*, 1919

Juan Gris: *Le Canigou*, 1921

Three Musicians, 1921

Like *Family of Saltimbanques* and *Les Demoiselles d'Avignon*, Picasso's *Three Musicians* (shown here in the two versions that he produced simultaneously) represents a summing up. The pictures reflect his long involvement with Cubism and look forward to the deft manipulations of form and color that would occupy him throughout his career. Here, in a retrospective glance, two figures from an earlier period reappear: Harlequin, the diamond-suited figure playing a guitar in the picture at right and a violin *(above)*, and Pierrot, the white-costumed clown who plays a recorder in both pictures. The third figure is a masked monk, who appears to sing from a sheet of music *(right)* and who holds a concertina *(above)*. A shaggy dog, whose dark shadow is projected on the background and left-hand wall *(right)*, is missing from the other version. Dazzling color has returned to Picasso's palette here; it dances across the surface on a jigsaw puzzle of circles, triangles and rectangles. And mood has returned as well; a nocturnal eeriness pervades these pictures and a sense of fantasy is strong. In this mature Cubist work, the introduction of fantasy and dream point the way to Picasso's future.

Three Musicians, 1921

V

Years of Trial

After 14 years, Picasso's marriage to Olga was plainly headed for the rocks. They could no longer gloss over their differences in temperament and taste; open clashes erupted between mercurial husband and strong-willed wife. Picasso decided that Olga had no real interest in his painting; her attentions seemed almost obsessively fixed on the social ladder. Once amused by her ambitions, he now found them intolerable. "She asked too much of me," he said long afterward.

Olga's regard for the proprieties kept her side of the story untold, but a few intelligent guesses can be ventured. Picasso's avowed desire was to "live like a poor man with a great deal of money." While this urge to cling to Bohemia in the midst of luxury had a certain perverse charm in theory, in practice it was bound to outrage his conventional wife. She had a more concrete cause for annoyance in any event: in the winter of 1931, the sensuous figure and features of an unknown young woman suddenly burst across Picasso's canvases.

His new model—and also his mistress—was a 21-year-old German girl, Marie-Thérèse Walter, whom he had met simply by engaging her in conversation on the street outside a Paris department store. She was as different from Olga as possible. Olga was a petite brunette; Marie-Thérèse was a big blonde. She was as earthy as Olga was patrician, as indolent as Olga was energetic, as easygoing as Olga was tight-lipped. Curiously, she shared Olga's apathy toward art; her only known enthusiasm was for sports. Picasso seemed all the more enchanted by her indifference to his work and his celebrity, and he throve under her unfailing good humor. Marie-Thérèse was not one to put a halter on a man. Whenever he turned up long past the promised hour at her apartment, she would greet him no less affably. "Eh Pablo," she would say, "you're late, as usual."

Marie-Thérèse's arrival on the scene inspired an entire series of paintings of which she is the subject, seen frankly and lustily through the eyes of a lover more than twice her age. Most of the pictures show her at rest, with her head folded in her arms, her body voluptuous, her mouth inviting, her eyes gently candid or serenely quiet and sometimes closed as if in sleep. All the paintings pay forthright tribute to her fair hair and skin and ample proportions. Picasso's own favorite, *The Girl Before a Mirror (page 123)*, is full of subtle complexities, as if the artist had paused in the midst of his enjoyment of immediate pleasures to ponder the outcome for the future.

Picasso's theme—a woman looking at her reflection—had impressive artistic credentials. Both Titian and Rubens had painted a nude Venus in rapt contemplation of her mirrored charms. Manet had modernized the theme, showing a woman in contemporary dress. But while Manet's woman is naturalistic, her mirror image has dissolved so that nothing is apparent but paint itself; this invokes the old puzzle of what is real and what is illusion. Picasso built on Manet's idea of producing an image that unrealistically reflects the figure before the mirror, but each of Picasso's figures is as real, or as illusory, as the other. They present, in fact, a study in split personality. The girl in front of the mirror looks relatively innocent and childlike; the image is older, with a dark aura and sultry gaze and a stance that flaunts her nakedness.

Picasso used a whole spectrum of vivid colors—among others, red, yellow, purple, green and orange—and set them off with thick black lines, much as a medieval craftsman leaded the stained-glass windows of a Gothic cathedral. This same effect had appeared in recent still lifes by Picasso, but its use in the dual portrait of Marie-Thérèse may have been meant to conjure up the notion of a latter-day Madonna. The impression is strengthened by the noticeably protruding bellies of both the girl and the image. In this sense Picasso's painting had the gift of prophecy: three years after its completion, Marie-Thérèse was to bear him a child, a fair-haired daughter they named María Concepción and called Maya for short.

By any conventional standards, *The Girl Before a Mirror* hardly meets the norm of beauty established by its prototype, Titian's *Venus with the Mirror*. Picasso was always impatient with the idea that any such norm should exist. Christian Zervos, who painstakingly catalogued Picasso's works, once raised the question with him and drew an irate answer. "The beauties of the Parthenon, the Venuses, the Nymphs, the Narcissuses, are so many lies," said Picasso. "Art is not the application of a canon of beauty, but what the instinct and the brain can conceive independently of that canon. When you love a woman you don't take instruments to measure her body, you love her with your desires."

Looking back over these early years of Picasso's involvement with Marie-Thérèse, one of his biographers observed that Picasso had taken her on a trip "through the successive stages of his art." Ever eager to evoke her supple eroticism, he glorified her not only in paint but in sculpture and etchings.

In the studios at Boisgeloup where he worked in the summer of 1932—high-ceilinged coach houses had become sculpture workshops—Picasso worked intensively at rendering Marie-Thérèse in all her robust three dimensions. He made a number of plaster studies of her body, her head and bust, and her head alone. Many of the heads—massive works, some of them six feet high—were later cast in bronze. The

Marie-Thérèse Walter, the serene young woman who inspired much of Picasso's happier work in the 1930s, poses here with pigeons that the artist gave her not long after they met. Always a source of pleasure and a happy reminder of his boyhood days in Spain, the pigeons were a most appropriate gift to Marie-Thérèse, whose calm, unruffled nature soothed the artist during the breakup of his marriage to Olga.

Mythological monsters appear throughout Picasso's collection of graphic works entitled the *Vollard Suite*, named after Ambroise Vollard, the publisher and art dealer who commissioned the book's 100 pictures. This grotesque creature is an amalgam of a female griffin and a Minotaur (half-man, half-bull). Like many of Picasso's monsters, it appears both menacing and harmless. Here, the children seem to be more curious about the beast than fearful of it.

first heads were Classical, showing Marie-Thérèse in a mood of repose, with idealized yet recognizable features, including her remarkable high-bridged nose. Later heads were less simply executed and somewhat metamorphic, with a receding forehead, jutting nose and elongated neck. On some of these heads the eyes bulge out as if affixed ex post facto; on others the eyes are incised, slitlike.

Picasso's greatest single testament to his love for Marie-Thérèse, however, appeared in a series of etchings called *The Sculptor's Studio*. For several years he had been under contract to supply illustrations for Vollard, who had long before added a publishing venture to his activities as a picture dealer. Over a 10-year period ending in 1937, Picasso was to turn out 100 engravings and etchings for Vollard, some single works, others sets, together making up what is now known as the *Vollard Suite*. *The Sculptor's Studio* was one of the sets—46 plates in all. Of these Picasso produced 40 in about six weeks in the spring of 1933, and the remaining six the following year.

The special challenges of etching technique had long intrigued Picasso; the dexterity and precision of line it required had been his since youth. In the past he had experimented with the medium only occasionally; once, during the Rose Period, he had turned out a series of 14 etchings of harlequins and other circus characters—an effort mainly intended to earn him a few badly needed francs. Now, in the prime of his career and at the height of his liaison with Marie-Thérèse, he conceived the idea of summing up both phases of his life—his art and his love affair—in a single allegorical sequence that would employ the clarity and simplicity of etched line.

The 46 scenes of *The Sculptor's Studio*—done with utmost delicacy in Neo-Classical style—were the stunning result. The protagonists are a bearded sculptor and his statuesque model, who are also obviously lovers. Sometimes they stand, sometimes they lie together, always they touch; their unity is seemingly complete. Yet they never look directly at each other; their glances, sometimes solemn, sometimes anxious, turn toward a third presence: the sculptor's work. From scene to scene the sculpture may be a horse, two horses gamboling, a bull attacking a horse, or a bull bearing a girl across its back. Whatever the third presence, it is an intrusion into the lovers' idyll, and perhaps an augury that they will never find true peace together.

Another sequence in the *Vollard Suite* paved the way for Picasso's greatest work. These etchings featured a minotaur, in Classical mythology a monstrous creature, half bull and half man, who periodically devoured seven maidens and seven youths sent him as tribute. The Surrealists, searching for new symbols to express the ills of the 1930s, had hit upon the minotaur as a symbol of human bestiality and the violence of the modern age. Picasso amended the symbolism; as if to say that the brutishness of human society was as mindless as the forces of nature, he made the minotaur innocent in his destructiveness.

Picasso's etchings take the minotaur through a series of encounters with humankind: artists and their models, the spectators at a bullfight, fishermen, children. Despite the minotaur's overwhelming power, his muscular body and his menacing horns, his eyes often have a gentle look. Sometimes he is playful, and nuzzles the people he is with. Sometimes he wounds them, but he appears to do so unwittingly. Toward the end of the series the minotaur becomes blind. In this stricken state, he is at his most bestial and most terrifying.

Picasso soon expanded on the theme in an unusually large etching— 19½ by 27¼ inches—entitled *Minotauromachy*, the "war of the minotaur" *(page 134)*. In this work the monster, sprung from the sea, reaches his menacing arm toward a little girl, who fearlessly greets him with a bouquet and a candle to light his way. Behind the child a man climbs a ladder, fleeing for his life. Above her two women lean on a window sill; they are intent on watching two doves, and are oblivious to both the minotaur and the danger of the child. Between the child and the minotaur a woman in matador dress, wounded by the minotaur, slips dying from a horse he has gored and disemboweled. The dying woman impotently clutches her sword, its tip pointed futilely away from the minotaur. The human attributes of strength and frailty, gentleness and brutality, courage and fear, indifference and innocence are all here, and Picasso has pitted one against another with dramatic urgency. The horrors foreseen in the *Minotauromachy* were soon to become a reality, and Picasso's masterpiece, *Guernica*, would record them for history.

In the summer of 1935, Picasso stayed in Paris—the first time he had done so in 30 years. Although he was ordinarily a poor correspondent, he now wrote to his old friend Sabartés in Spain: "I am alone in the house. You can imagine what has happened and what is waiting for me." He and Olga had finally parted; she had gone off with their son Paulo, leaving him alone on the Rue La Boétie. Marie-Thérèse and her infant daughter lived in an apartment elsewhere in Paris, and Picasso visited them regularly. Little Maya had Marie-Thérèse's blonde hair, blue eyes and good health, and signs of her father's Spanish temperament. She delighted him as Paulo had. Sabartés was to

Jaime Sabartés, Picasso's oldest and closest friend, shown above in a 1943 photograph, has been a willing subject for the artist since their youth in Barcelona. But never was he quite the same subject twice. Some of the many guises and styles in which Picasso depicted his amigo are shown on the opposite page. At the top, Sabartés peers wistfully over his tall beer glass. Below, he is an elegant gentleman with a mustache and steel-rimmed spectacles. The two lower drawings cast Sabartés in the role of a 16th Century Spanish cavalier and of a mythical pipe-playing satyr. On this last picture, Picasso has written Sabartés' first name in Latin and the place where he drew the portrait in Greek —Antipolis is Antibes, on the Riviera.

record of this new chapter in Picasso's parenthood that "one day, being absolutely determined to do something different, he set to washing diapers—that, at least, had nothing whatsoever to do with his previous occupations." Picasso talked with lawyers; evidently he thought of divorcing Olga and marrying Marie-Thérèse. But Spain does not recognize divorce, and Picasso did not wish to give up his Spanish citizenship, so he did not pursue the matter.

He began to feel at loose ends, and in the fall went to the château at Boisgeloup. In his unaccustomed solitude there he undertook a new pursuit—writing poetry. Perhaps he was reaching out for a new form of expression to compensate for the upheaval in his life, and he took to jotting Surrealistic verse in a small notebook he carried in his pocket. He tried to keep this a secret, but somehow word reached Barcelona and his mother, who wrote him: "They tell me that you write. I can believe anything of you. If one day they tell me that you say Mass, I shall believe it just the same."

He was unbearably lonely, and at last he wrote Sabartés asking that he come to Paris and share his apartment. Sabartés not only came; he lived with Picasso or nearby for years, and faithfully served as secretary, watchdog, companion and confidant.

Sabartés found the spacious apartment on the Rue La Boétie a jumble of canvases, unanswered mail and assorted oddments. Picasso would never discard or even disturb whatever accumulated around him. "I cannot explain your mania for keeping things," Sabartés said, "considering you are an innovator by temperament." Picasso protested: "Why should you want me to throw away what has done me the favor of coming into my hands?"

Picasso showed his poetry to Sabartés, and with his encouragement showed it to others. It was written in Spanish, but he read it aloud and translated it into French. The Surrealists among his listeners particularly approved. Picasso's poetry was spontaneous and unselfconscious, unfettered by rules of grammar or form; yet it was full of original imagery. One poem begins:

> "give wrench twist and kill I make my way set alight and burn caress
> and lick embrace and watch I ring at full peal the bells . . ."

Several of Picasso's poems appeared during the winter of 1935-1936 in the influential magazine *Cahiers d'Art.*

Despite his new pride of authorship and the company of Sabartés and other friends, Picasso could not keep from brooding over the impasse in his private life. He sank into a state of despair. His caprices hardened into habits, and bursts of temper grew more explosive. He had always been cranky about visitors when he was working; now he might refuse to see anyone at any time for any reason, and Sabartés was at the door to send callers away. Picasso had always been careless of promises; now they meant nothing. Vollard often had to wait months for engravings he had contracted for, and so did buyers for paintings. Most of Picasso's friends detected a change in him; once overwhelming in his vitality, now he seemed to be in a coma.

1901

1904

1938

1946

Sabartés later recalled that during this period Picasso "refused to set foot in his studio. The mere sight of his pictures and drawings exasperated him, for every one of them recalled something of his recent past and every memory was an unhappy one." Gertrude Stein added that Picasso "ceased to paint in 1935. In fact he ceased to paint during two years and he neither painted nor drew. . . . It was very curious." Her statement was picked up and retold as gospel, but it was not true. Although Picasso was in a sullen mood, he never ceased to paint. Between 1935 and 1937 he produced a great many portraits of Marie-Thérèse—but he never offered them for sale, and for several years he did not even show them to anyone.

For all his isolation, Picasso made one important new friend: Paul Éluard, the Surrealist poet. They had met casually at the end of World War I, but now began to see a good deal of each other. In the coming years they would communicate even when Picasso buried himself so deeply in silent gloom that he shut out the rest of the world.

As always when forging a friendship, Picasso paid tribute to Éluard by producing his portrait—in this case with a pencil drawing of spare lines that realistically depict the poet's high forehead and pensive look. Some months later, he made several etchings for a book of Éluard's verse, in which he depicted the poet's wife, Nusch, a woman watching

In 1936 Picasso mixed his styles in making illustrations for a book of surrealist verse written by Paul Éluard. While the poet watched, Picasso marked off a copper plate into four parts and drew a head of Nusch, Éluard's wife *(at the upper left)*. Next to it he etched a mysterious, half-hieroglyphic scene, and below that he added his mistress, Marie-Thérèse, napping out of doors. In the fourth quarter—which was not used in the book—Picasso playfully inked his own right hand and pressed it on the plate. (It looks like his left hand because the printing of an etching reverses its image.)

a sunburst and the sleeping head of Marie-Thérèse. The two friends subsequently worked together on other books, Éluard writing the poetry and Picasso engraving the illustrations.

Éluard, in turn, was to serve Picasso well. Like the poet Apollinaire before him, he sounded the praises of Picasso's art far and wide. In the spring of 1936, a group of young Spanish painters and poets—the Amigos de las Artes Nuevas (Friends of the New Arts)—organized a retrospective Picasso show, the first in his native land since a brief display of his early works in Barcelona in 1901. Wishing to oblige his countrymen, Picasso sent a number of paintings still in his possession to add to those lent by collectors. He took a great deal of trouble over details of mailing and insurance that he ordinarily neglected. He did not, however, attend the exhibition, which appeared in Barcelona, Madrid and Bilbao. Éluard went as his deputy and lectured at the opening.

There were also three shows of Picasso's work in Paris early that year—an exhibit of his drawings, another of his sculptures, and another of his paintings. The paintings were shown at Paul Rosenberg's gallery, next door to Picasso's apartment. Picasso found himself besieged with curiosity-seekers who discovered, as Rosenberg had, that it was easy to catch sight of him through his bathroom window.

To escape the prying eyes Picasso went off to Juan-les-Pins on the Riviera. Although he had gone off freely on vacations with his earlier loves, this was one of the few times he ever openly spent a holiday with Marie-Thérèse. Seeking anonymity, he asked Sabartés to forward his mail in the name of "Pablo Ruiz." But Picasso was restless, and after about eight weeks returned to Paris. He set to work to fulfill a long-due promise to Vollard to provide illustrations for a new edition of the Comte de Buffon's *Histoire Naturelle*, an 18th Century tome that despite its outdated zoological information has remained a classic of French literature. Choosing the birds and animals that appealed to him among the species mentioned in Buffon's work, Picasso produced 31 aquatints in all, delicate and minutely observed.

In the course of the project he journeyed every day to the shop of the printer Roger Lacourière, whom Vollard had engaged, traveling up the steep hills of Montmartre to the environs of his first home in Paris. With his insatiable curiosity, Picasso plied Lacourière's crew of printers with questions about the technical processes they used. Together they completed the aquatints at the rate of one a day although the book itself was not published until after Vollard's death in 1939.

With the completion of this work, Picasso returned to the south, this time to Mougins, to spend the rest of the summer with Éluard and his wife. One day at luncheon with a friend at nearby St. Tropez, he met a black-haired, green-eyed girl to whom Éluard had introduced him some months before. Her name was Dora Maar, and she was intelligent, vivacious and aristocratic. Her father, a Yugoslavian architect, had taken the family to live in Argentina, so she had the advantage of being able to converse with Picasso in his own language. At St. Tropez, Picasso took her for a walk after lunch, then asked her to return to Mougins with him—which she did.

Dora Maar, shown here relaxing with Picasso in 1937 on the beach at Golfe-Juan, a Riviera town near Mougins, was the fourth of the six women important to his life. Like the others, she served as a stimulus to his art, appearing frequently as the subject of portraits in the late '30s and early '40s.

Dora's first appearance in Picasso's work was a witty drawing—obviously a play on the difference in their ages—which shows her, dressed for a trip, opening a door and finding herself face-to-face with a bearded old man holding a dog in his lap. Dora became the new "first woman" in Picasso's life. For the next decade she was to dominate his pictures as her predecessors had done. Marie-Thérèse continued, as always, to exist in the background.

The encounter with Dora lifted Picasso from his torpor. If his personal affairs improved, however, events elsewhere took a turn for the worse. Spain was torn by civil war. Picasso, still strongly attached to his native land after 30 years away from it, could not remain unmoved.

The Spanish government of the time, the Second Republic, represented the second phase of a struggling democracy that had supplanted the centuries-old monarchy in 1931. Its hold on the reins of power was at best tenuous, and the country itself remained essentially feudal in character. Spain lagged far behind the rest of Western Europe economically. Many peasants subsisted abominably; they tilled tiny plots on large estates and were subject to eviction at the will of their landlords. Industry was still in its infancy; where it existed, the worker was virtually a serf. Aristocratic landowners and parvenu industrialists had the support of the Church and the army, and together these four influential blocs aimed to perpetuate their own interests.

The Second Republic had come into being with the help of professionals and middle-class people like Picasso's parents. But they had failed to make it function effectively. Desperately needed agrarian and industrial reforms waited while the Republic's supporters splintered into factions; in one of the issues at stake, some clamored for strong centralized rule, others for local autonomy. The government was further beset by anarchists much like those Picasso had known at Els Quatre Gats at the turn of the century. Very few reforms could be effected. Peasants, workers and intellectuals remained unsatisfied, and the Republic grew weaker.

Discontent had mounted for five years. Now elections in February 1936 brought in a so-called Popular Front government, composed not only of Republicans, but of Communists, Socialists, and even anarchists. Although this government instituted some reforms, the people wanted more radical measures. A series of work stoppages spread through Madrid's industrial plants; by July, Spain's major cities had suffered some 300 strikes. Riots followed the strikes. Homes were sacked, monasteries and churches were burned; prisoners were turned loose from jails, and newspaper publications were severely curtailed as each faction vented its hostilities.

On July 13 a conservative member of the *Cortes*, the Parliament, was assassinated. A small band of army officers in Spanish Morocco seized upon this incident as an excuse to revolt against the Popular Front government and its projected reforms. The insurrection spread to garrisons in Spain, and the rebels in uniform were joined by police and right-wingers. The government, loyal soldiers and trade unionists fought back, and within a few days civil war raged across Spain.

By October the Rebel Army had laid siege to the government in Madrid, and was in control of nearly half of the country. Its leader was Generalissimo Francisco Franco, a man with a talent for keeping his political opinions to himself, and, consequently, a brilliant record of advancement at the hands of the old monarchist government. Franco had been the youngest captain, the youngest major, the youngest colonel, and the youngest general in the Spanish Army. On October 1, at the age of 43, he proclaimed himself Head of State. In the area of the country where he ruled—"Nationalist" Spain—he halted such meager reforms as the Second Republic had got under way, squashed the opposition of intellectuals and the protests of peasants and workers and installed a military dictatorship.

Franco's coup d'état was possible because the Loyalist government was weak and public opinion divided. But the very division of sentiment nourished and sustained resistance, and the civil war raged on. While the democracies stood on the sidelines, Nazi Germany and Fascist Italy put bombs, planes and men at Franco's disposal; the Soviet Union supplied arms to the Republicans and required its workers to donate one half of one per cent of their monthly wages to the cause.

Ever since his youth Picasso had offered his own artistic commentaries on social and human ills—among them his cartoons for the magazine *Arte Joven* in Madrid in 1901, his poverty-stricken people of the Blue Period paintings, and more recently his ominous Minotaur series. But he had always kept aloof from politics as such. Now, however, because of his abiding affection for Spain and his sympathies for the ordinary man, he could not be indifferent.

Recognizing Picasso's international stature, the Amigos de las Artes Nuevas persuaded the Republican government, beleaguered in Madrid, to name him director *in absentia* of the great Prado Museum. Although this was obviously a propaganda move, Picasso accepted in order to emphasize his support of the Republic. But fighting, bombing and arson soon made the city an inferno, and the Prado's masterpieces had to be removed to safety. "So I am director of an empty museum," Picasso said bitterly.

He had a personal as well as an ideological concern in the war. In Barcelona a convent was set ablaze next door to the apartment where his mother lived with his sister, Lola, now widowed, and Lola's five children. Señora Ruiz and her daughter and grandchildren were unharmed but for weeks afterward smoke and the odor of burned flesh permeated their apartment.

Picasso gave tirelessly to the Republican cause. He sold several paintings he had been keeping for himself, then turned over the money they brought for Spanish relief purposes. He also gave cash out of his pocket; one relief official estimated that Picasso had given a total of 400,000 francs to feed the hungry, additional sums to enable a variety of Spanish intellectuals to pursue their work, and numerous and generous private gifts to individuals.

His most memorable service to Republican Spain was to come in the year that followed, when he painted his masterwork *Guernica*.

In the spring of 1917, Picasso traveled to Rome to design the sets and costumes for Jean Cocteau's ballet *Parade*, which was being produced by Sergei Diaghilev, the great impresario of the Ballets Russes. Rome and the ballet came as a breath of fresh air to the artist. While there he met his first wife, Olga Khokhlova, a dancer. And after nine years of almost complete immersion in Cubism he turned again to painting and drawing the human figure realistically. Some of these works are delicate and lyrical. In others, perhaps inspired by the dramatic architecture, overwhelming monuments and colossal sculptures of Rome, Picasso began to breed on canvas a weighty, statuesque race of people like the casually draped, seated lady at the right.

For a few years these gentle forms occupied him. But then, in 1925, his mood changed again. He began to demonize the figure, manipulating the human form into exaggerated, angular distortions with bestial features. Was it Sigmund Freud's startling views of the hidden scenes of men's minds that caused the change—views that revolutionized contemporary thought and inspired Surrealism as an art form? Was it increasing tension in a depressed Europe? Was it the anticipated breakup of his marriage to Olga? Probably all these causes and many more interacted. But Picasso was alert, keenly observant, sensitive to change. During this period, as always, his art was his own response to the world around him.

Goddesses and Grotesques

Her face devoid of emotion, her enormous body rooted to the earth, Picasso's gigantic seated woman is a symbol of universal fertility. Her massive, chiseled features reflect the artist's interest in Classical Roman statuary.

Seated Woman, 1920

Portrait of Olga in an Armchair, 1917

As the circus and its performers had captivated Picasso during his Rose Period, so now, as he worked on *Parade*, he became entranced by the ballet. This fascination with graceful beauty and the theater is evident in the drawing below, which captures in fluid lines the dancelike attitudes of 15 nude bathers. It is also clear in the costume sketch at right, whose characters are so reminiscent of earlier circus paintings. The sketch was a costume design for a later production of the Ballets Russes, Igor Stravinsky's charming *Pulcinella*.

While these drawings seem quite realistic, they also reveal Picasso's continuing involvement with Cubism. The flat outlined shapes strongly resemble those of the bottles, bowls and fruit of his still lifes. Similarly, in his portrait of his future wife, Olga *(left)*, Picasso has painted the tapestry-covered chair on which she sits as if it were a piece of cloth pinned to the flat wall, one of the techniques of collage. And although Olga's figure is well-modeled, the background is so loosely brushed and raw that she too seems to have been painted separately and then pasted, like a cutout, onto the canvas. The experience of Cubism was still very much with Picasso.

Pierrot and Harlequin, 1918

The Bathers, 1918

COLLECTION PICASSO

Pipes of Pan, 1923

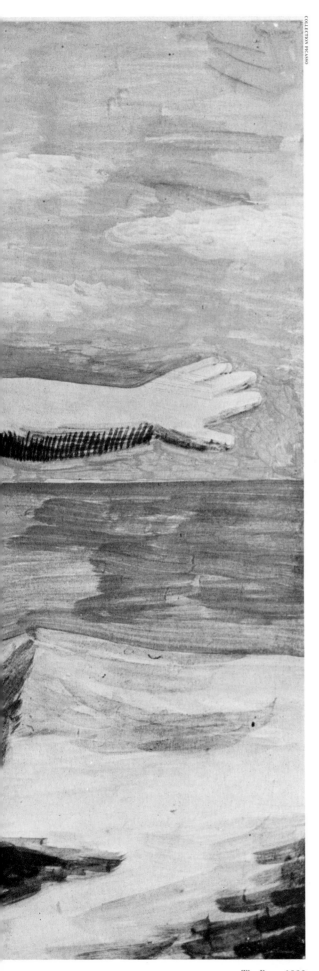

COLLECTION PICASSO

The Race, 1922

Picasso's experience of Rome and the wealth of Imperial art he saw there had a profound effect on his style. He found in the majestic stone sculptures of men and women—muscular athletes, robust warriors, draped goddesses—a sense of grandeur that he applied in his own portrayals of the human figure. In the paintings shown here, Picasso also combined his current interest in the theater, stimulated by the ballet, with the monumental forms of Roman antiquity. The two huge bathers above appear against a timeless setting of sea and sky, posed between jutting forms as if between the sides of a theater's proscenium arch. Before a similar seaside backdrop, the giantesses at the left race along a shore in happy abandon. So ponderous that their earthshaking footfalls seem almost audible, the women nonetheless have the lithe mobility of ballet dancers. The striking, theatrical quality of this particular picture ultimately came to good use. In greatly enlarged form, it became the drop curtain for the Ballets Russes production of a new work, *Le Train Bleu*, named for the crack express between Paris and the Riviera. The theme of the ballet was the fun and frolics of genteel society at the seashore; beach sports inspired the dances. And Picasso's enormous racing figures must have made a stunning impression on the waiting audience.

117

Three Graces, 1924

Few pictures painted at virtually the same time in an artist's life could be more dissimilar than these two. The elegant, long-limbed ladies above, posed in a variation of the attitudes of the Three Graces, are the last of Picasso's serene, Classical figures. At right, the diabolical dance of distorted forms in *The Three Dancers* signals the beginning of a new and extraordinary period in his art. In 1925, Picasso began to rip the human body apart, dislocating arms, noses, breasts, mouths. This was no careful, geometric analysis of form such as he had undertaken in his Cubist works. Rather, it seemed to be a dissection of a mental state. Perhaps in reaction to disillusionments in his marriage, Picasso saw everything in terms of some anxious nightmare.

The Three Dancers, 1925

Woman in an Armchair, 1929

The destruction of the human figure, begun with *The Three Dancers*, gathered momentum in the years that followed. Picasso concentrated almost exclusively on a single subject—a seated woman, tranquilly posed but violently treated. And he attacked her in an extraordinary range of styles, each uncovering a terrifying aspect.

Splintered faces, simultaneous profile and front views, animalistic features and hard, hot colors generate terror in these pictures. At the left, a woman with a gaping jaw filled with sharklike teeth utters an almost audible shriek. At the right, a similarly posed figure is calmer and more solidly proportioned, but her bared teeth reveal a glimpse of brutality just beneath the surface. Directly below are other menacing females of this period: at the far right, a touch of whimsy seems to have entered Picasso's view, yet the figure is laughing with diabolical glee.

Seated Bather, 1930

Seated Woman, 1927

Figure in a Red Chair, 1932

The Yellow Belt, 1932

The Dream, 1932

In 1932, Picasso's vengeful attack on the female figure abated. He had become interested in a new woman and the lift in his spirits is evident in these two pictures. The torment of earlier works is gone, although an unsettling quality remains. Above, the face and body of the girl asleep are curiously halved, perhaps to suggest the dual reality of dream and waking. At the right, the woman's mirror image seems to be her mysterious other self.

122

Girl Before a Mirror, 1932

123

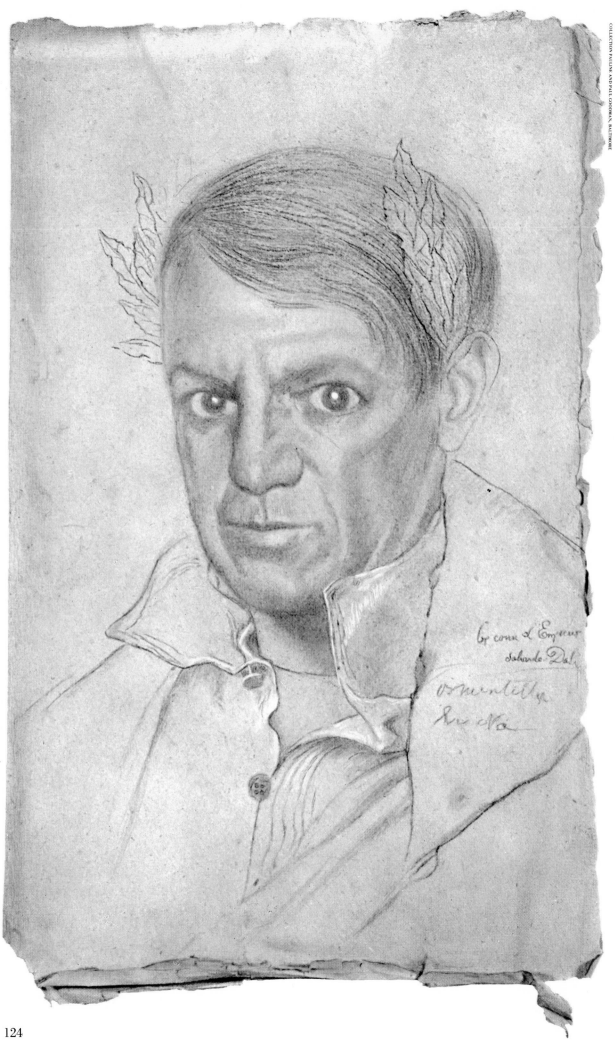

VI

"Painting...is an instrument of war"

Picasso's sympathies in the Spanish Civil War were shared by most creative artists, whether or not they shared his attachment to Spain itself. Even the nonpolitical among them detected the threat to the creative spirit in the totalitarian voice of Franco's Fascism. Seldom had a war received such energetic support from writers and painters the world over as the Spanish Republic's struggle for its life.

At one low ebb in the Republicans' military fortunes, in January of 1937, Picasso gave vent to his feelings in his art. With Franco as his direct target, he produced a set of etchings that lampooned the dictator as a grotesque creature like a cancerous, hairy turnip, wearing a crown and grinning evilly from a mouth in its middle. This arrogant monster —unlike any Picasso had yet devised, and certainly the most repulsive —tilts at the sun, slaughters a horse, axes a statue. In some scenes only the victims appear. Mostly they are women and children, dead, dying or hopelessly despairing.

Picasso engraved this savagery in two large copper plates, each of which he divided into nine rectangles about the size of postcards. Originally he intended to have the 18 etchings sold separately, to raise money for the Republican cause. But their combined effect was so powerful that it was decided to present them as a series with the scenes arranged in sequence, like the "Alleluia" he had sketched in 1904 on the occasion of his journey to settle in Paris.

He also decided to add a poem of his own composing, written in the Surrealist style of his earlier verse. If his verbal images were less successful than those he had etched, they still reflected his loathing of an unnamed tyrant:

> fandango of shivering owls souse of swords of evil-omened polyps scouring brush of hairs from priests' tonsures standing naked in the middle of the frying-pan placed upon the ice-cream cone of codfish fried in the scabs of his lead-ox heart . . .

The etchings and the poem, reproduced in Picasso's handwriting, appeared in the form of an album entitled *The Dream and Lie of Franco.*

This previously unpublished drawing by the Surrealist Dali both pays homage to Picasso and pokes a little well-aimed fun at him. The laurel wreath around his head—or is it a set of devilish horns—seems to be Dali's joke at his celebrated rival's expense. But whether in praise or derision, Dali has captured Picasso's features with exactness.

Salvador Dali: *Portrait of Picassso*, 1933

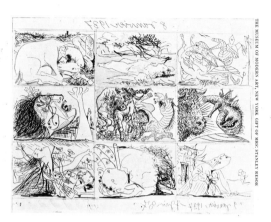

To help the cause of the Spanish Republican government during the civil war, Picasso designed 18 etchings that, accompanied by an impassioned poem, he called *The Dream and Lie of Franco*. Incised on two plates, one of which is shown above, the etchings depicted Franco in grotesque forms. In the climactic picture, enlarged below, the dictator becomes a horselike creature disemboweled by a bull.

This was just the opening gun of his personal campaign. Even before this damning portfolio could be issued, the Spanish Republic called upon Picasso the propagandist for a larger effort: a mural which was to be the major adornment of its pavilion at the Paris World's Fair in the summer of 1937.

Picasso promptly accepted the assignment. Since his own studio at the Rue La Boétie was not large enough to accommodate his work on the project, he rented two floors in a 17th Century house on the Rue des Grands-Augustins, near the Seine. For several months he procrastinated, painting decorative still lifes and portraits of Marie-Thérèse and his new love, Dora Maar. These pictures betray no sign of conflict; it was as if he had deliberately put the war out of his mind.

Picasso was shaken into action by a single event in Spain. On April 26, 1937, German bombers flying for Franco wiped out the small Basque town of Guernica. They attacked at the busiest hour of a market day; the streets were jammed with townspeople and peasants in from the countryside. Never before in modern war had noncombatants been slaughtered in such numbers, and by such means. Worse still, Guernica had no strategic value for Franco's armies, but it had a poignant meaning for 600,000 Basques: from the early Middle Ages onward, it had been a kind of capital for the Basques, symbolizing their independent spirit and democratic ideals.

Within a week an unfuriated Picasso was at work at his mural. In just the first 10 days he made about 25 sketches: of bulls, of slain horses, of a woman leaning from a window with a lantern, of other figures, separately and in groups. On the 11th day he set up a gigantic canvas, about 25 feet long and 11 feet high. The room in which he worked was just long enough to accommodate the canvas, but not, despite the old-fashioned ceilings, high enough. Undaunted, Picasso placed the canvas at a slant. As he painted he would climb up and down a ladder, moving it in short hauls the length of the room as he went; where the canvas slanted away from his reach he employed a special long-handled brush, leaning precariously forward from his ladder perch. He had an enthralled audience in his new mistress. Dora not only kept him company but photographed the work as it progressed.

In about a month of unremitting labor Picasso completed his great *Guernica (pages 137-139)*. It may well be the most terrifying document on the horrors of war ever to be produced by an artist. In it, Picasso marshaled many of the techniques he had employed in previous years: the flat, fragmented figures of Cubism; the dislocations of eyes, ears, profiles, limbs; the powerful, abstracted forms of primitive African art; the symbols of his Minotaur series. But the artistic means Picasso used pale in importance alongside the end he achieved; *Guernica* is a monumental outcry of human grief at its most anguished.

The central figure is a wounded horse, its head upraised in a paroxysm of fright. Above it is a sun shaped like an eye with an electric bulb for a pupil; below his hooves lies a slain warrior, one hand clutching a broken sword, the other tautly outflung. To the left a bull looks off into the distance. Below him a woman holding a dead child sends a shriek heavenward. At the right are three other women. One falls screaming from a burning house, her clothes aflame. Another runs in mindless flight. The third, represented only by a head and an arm, thrusts forth a lamp.

The final painting contained a number of important changes from Picasso's earlier conceptions of it. In preliminary sketches the bull looked toward the center of the picture; by reversing its head Picasso made it seem to be scanning an unseen horizon. The fallen warrior originally raised a clenched fist in the leftist salute of the Spanish Popular Front. At the start Picasso had planned an outdoor scene, but he added such indoor effects as the light bulb, the tiled floor, a table and suggestions of the contours of a room.

Perhaps the most important change was his decision to paint *Guernica* solely in black, gray and white. These somber hues, unrelieved in any way, emphasize the tragedy. Neither in the colors, nor in the figures, nor in all the complex symbolism of the painting, is there hope. Even the woman's lamp only serves to illumine calamity.

Picasso is usually loath to expound on his pictures, but in 1944, after Allied troops liberated Paris in World War II, he explained *Guernica's* two most important symbols to an American soldier who interviewed him at his studio. "The bull," Picasso said, "is not fascism, but it is brutality and darkness. . . . The horse represents the people."

By Picasso's own account the bull would seem to be the villain of the piece. Yet some critics have suggested that even in the "brutality and darkness" of which Picasso spoke, the creature is as guiltless as the victims, and that in surveying the horizon it is no less bewildered than the frantic horse and the screaming women. If, indeed, the bull is not the villain, then the enemy is nowhere on the canvas—an omission that conveys a chilling message: to the victims of modern warfare, the enemy remains impersonal and unknown.

In a matter of weeks after Picasso finished his giant mural it was mounted on a wall inside the entrance of the Spanish pavilion at the World's Fair. It touched off a storm of controversy. Picasso was taken to task on political as well as artistic grounds. Franco supporters, of course, vociferously attacked it, all the more so after a statement by Picasso was published saying that *Guernica* was intended to express his "abhorrence of the military caste which has sunk Spain in an ocean of pain and death." Less predictably, however, *Guernica* irked many partisans of the Republican cause, who felt that Picasso might better have expended his energy on a forthright call to arms.

The art critics were as divided as the political factions. One protester denounced the mural's "scarecrow figures," and another its "banality of overstatement." A distinguished champion of *Guernica*, the British critic Herbert Read, took up this charge. "Picasso's symbols are banal," Read wrote, "like the symbols of Homer, Dante, Cervantes. For it is only when the widest commonplace is inspired with the intensest passion that a great work of art, transcending all schools and categories, is born; and being born lives immortally." A more immediate note of prophecy appeared in an article in the magazine

At 4:40 in the afternoon of April 26, 1937, in an unprovoked attack, German pilots flying planes like the Heinkel III *(above)* dropped their bombs on the small, undefended Basque town of Guernica. Later in the day more bombs were dropped by Junkers 52s, also supplied to Franco by Nazi Germany. The town was severely damaged *(below)* by these wanton blows and two days later fell to Franco's Nationalist forces without resistance.

Cahiers d'Art, which devoted almost an entire issue to *Guernica* soon after its public debut. The author of the article was Michel Leiris, whose wife was later to take over Daniel-Henry Kahnweiler's gallery when another world war forced Kahnweiler to flee France for the second time in his life. Leiris wrote: "Picasso sends us our announcement of our mourning: all we love is going to die."

In just two years, the horrors of *Guernica* were to be incalculably compounded by a war that would engulf first Europe and then the globe. In the uneasy interim, the statesmen of France and England tried to curb or cajole the power-mad Führer of Germany, Adolf Hitler; as their efforts momentarily succeeded, or more often failed, the anxiety of Europeans still beyond Hitler's reach fell or rose accordingly. There was no hiding place from the headlines, and few were exempt from the tensions of the time. Picasso's art reflected the alternating currents of hope and fear. He created some of his gayest works, and some of his gloomiest, in these years.

He had little cause for personal complaint. Except for one frightening bout with sciatica, he was in fine health. His affair with Dora went well. She was not only good to look at, with her bright eyes and pert hairdo, but she was also good to talk to. Dora's camera record of Picasso's progressive revisions of *Guernica* was but one token of her eagerness to be a true helpmeet.

His prestige was skyrocketing. After the Paris World's Fair closed, *Guernica* went on tour—to Norway, to London and Liverpool, and across the Atlantic to New York. Picasso's name was beginning to have a familiar ring even to the random museum visitor. The proceeds of the *Guernica* showings went to the foundering Spanish Republican cause, but Picasso's other works brought him ever-larger sums. He had an elegant Hispano-Suiza, and a chauffeur, Marcel, to drive it when he traveled to the Riviera to spend the summers of 1937 and 1938 with Éluard and his wife at Mougins. Dora went along, of course, and so did a newer acquisition: an Afghan hound, Kazbek, named for a mountain in ancient Afghanistan. In his proud bearing and slender lines Kazbek proved strikingly compatible with the graceful Dora; the two of them, Picasso joked, were his most important models.

Dora alone inspired a host of portraits, some realistic, some distorted, some with her breasts defined in the spiral shapes of the spun sugar *torruellas* Picasso had drawn as a tot of two; in one impish mood, he placed her head atop a bird's body. The Éluards, too, came in for joshing. Picasso painted the poet's face over the body of a peasant woman nursing a cat, and his wife's face with two fish for eyes. He painted the men of the village of Mougins—and showed them ridiculously sucking lollipops. And yet, when there seemed no end to his playfulness, Picasso would turn around and produce veritable nightmares: a painting of a fiendish, half-human cat with a fluttering bird in its mouth *(page 140)*; a painting of a bull's head torn open to expose the bloody tissues, and perhaps most wrenching, a series of drawings of weeping women, successors to the tragic figures of *Guernica*.

Out of these fluctuations of mood came two of Picasso's most nota-

Until he moved to the south of France after World War II, Picasso habitually left Paris during the summer for the seashore. Most of the time he headed for the seven-mile stretch of Riviera coastline between Cannes and Antibes. Here he relaxes at a tree-shaded luncheon table in Mougins, just outside Cannes. With him are Dora Maar *(foreground, in shadow)* and Nusch Éluard, wife of Picasso's poet friend, Paul Éluard.

ble paintings. The *Woman Weeping (page 133)*, executed in Paris in the fall of 1937, goes far beyond her prototypes of *Guernica* and the drawings that followed. Human grief has never before or since sat for so stark a portrait: it becomes universal in the contorted mouth, the gnashing teeth, the maddened eyes. A handkerchief simultaneously covers and reveals the face; the tears are small ovals that serve also as clawing fingernails. Picasso's colors are the final, devastating touch: these are not the somber blacks and whites and grays of *Guernica*, but harsh and angry colors evoking pain and frenzy.

In the summer of 1939 Picasso painted *Night Fishing at Antibes*, a joyous bit of nonsense as cheering as the *Woman* is distressing. He and Dora had taken an apartment for the season at the little seaside resort, and despite the presence of newly mobilized soldiers in place of tourists, they were having a wonderful time. In the evening they would walk along the harborfront, munch double ice-cream cones, and watch the fishermen spearing their catch by the light of acetylene lamps. Picasso's translation of this scene is a triumph of genre in Cubist guise. Two fatuous girls on a jetty, one eating an ice-cream cone and balancing a bicycle at her side, goggle at two fishermen leaning out of a boat, intent on luring up the creatures of the deep. A spiral moon, in the shape of a spun sugar cake, hangs in the sky, and the hills and castle turrets of the town rise in the background.

The lighthearted mood that produced *Night Fishing* did not survive the drying of its paint. On September 1, just after Picasso finished the canvas, Hitler's armies invaded Poland. Two days later France and England, treaty-bound to defend Poland, declared war on Germany. Picasso and Dora took a train for Paris. They left Marcel to fill the Hispano-Suiza with their luggage and drive back to Paris. *Night Fishing at Antibes* traveled with him, rolled up on the back seat.

Picasso lingered in Paris only three days. Rumors flew that the city was to be bombed. Picasso, together with Dora and Kazbek, and Sabartés and his wife, drove to Royan, a small port on the Atlantic about 75 miles north of Bordeaux. They rented rooms and settled in.

Despite the jolt of the change, and the news that Éluard and other friends had been called up for military service, Picasso continued to paint and draw, almost furiously, as if to distract his thoughts. Materials were hard to come by; paper and sketchbooks were scarce, canvas more so. Even when he could get canvas, Picasso lacked an easel. He had to prop his work on a chair, use the seat of another chair for a palette, and make his own brushes. But the difficulties only spurred him on. He turned out scores of works, among them a portrait of Sabartés in a 16th Century ruff and plumed hat, with lopsided eyes and ears, and another portrait, *Woman Dressing Her Hair (page 141)*, that fused the features of Dora and Kazbek.

Except for three or four trips into Paris to try to get canvas or to place his paintings out of danger in bank vaults Picasso stayed in Royan until August of 1940, when German troops occupied the town. He returned to Paris and moved into the studio on the Rue des Grands-Augustins, where he had worked on *Guernica*. Although the American

One of Picasso's most familiar techniques in depicting the human form is the rearrangement of anatomy so that front, sides and sometimes the back appear simultaneously on the canvas. A carry-over from Cubism, such alteration is often seen in pictures like this 1937 ink-and-gouache drawing, in which Picasso places both eyes, brows and nostrils on the same side of the face in order to present the profile and front view at once.

and Mexican governments both offered him asylum, he was to remain there throughout the four-year Nazi occupation. "What shall we do with the Germans at our heels?" an artist asked him. "Hold exhibitions!" Picasso replied. But the Nazis forbade him to do so: Hitler scorned Picasso's work as degenerate "Bolshevik art."

The city was vastly changed. German soldiers were enjoying the cafés of Saint Germain-des-Prés that had in recent years replaced those of Montmartre and Montparnasse as the gathering place of Parisian intellectuals. A few of Picasso's ex-friends collaborated with the enemy. Some, like Éluard, were working in the underground resistance. Just as Picasso's tiny room at the *bateau lavoir* had been a Rendez-vous des Poètes nearly four decades earlier, so now his studio on the Rue des Grands-Augustins became a refuge for French friends existing precariously among the enemy.

The Nazis allowed Picasso the same freedom, such as it was, that they allowed the French. They did not molest him, but German officers called on him from time to time, at least once to solicit his collaboration. The grapevine carried several anecdotes about Picasso's response to Nazi overtures. One reported that Otto Abetz, the German Ambassador in Paris, offered to supply him with coal. Picasso refused, telling him coolly that "a Spaniard is never cold!" On leaving, Abetz was said to have noticed a photograph of *Guernica*, peered at it elaborately and exclaimed in recognition: "Ah Monsieur Picasso, so it was you who did that?" "No," Picasso retorted, "it was you." When he was asked about this story after the war, Picasso laughed and said, "Oh, it's true, more or less. The Boches used to visit me on the pretext of admiring my pictures. I gave them postcards of my canvas *Guernica* and told them: 'Take them away! Souvenir! Souvenir!'"

Often he was so cold that he worked bundled in sweaters, and wearing gloves with the fingers cut off. His pictures increasingly came to reflect the privations of war and the dearth of food and heat. Sometimes Picasso was so obsessed with hunger that he lovingly lavished representations of sausages and leeks on his canvases.

He made the most of the simplest materials that came to hand. On a walk one day in 1943, he found an abandoned bicycle. Picking up the saddle and the handlebars, he put them together in the form of a bull's head—one of his most ingenious and widely known metamorphoses. Picasso took particular pride in this work. Showing newspapermen through his studio after the liberation of Paris in 1944, he called special attention to it, and soon afterward he sent it to his first post-occupation exhibit. Another half-playful, half-serious work of 1943 was his painting *First Steps (page 156)*, showing the willful determination of a toddling child and the watchful concern of his mother. It was intended, perhaps, as a declaration that life persists in the midst of death.

During the Occupation, Picasso also created dozens of pieces of sculpture, modeling in plaster with his small, strong hands. None of his work could be cast though, because the Nazis had commandeered all metals, especially bronze, which they got by stripping and melting down some of Paris' celebrated statues—not to turn into cannon but

A special gift of Picasso's was his talent for investing familiar objects with totally new and often surprising identities. He created the sculpture *(above)* entitled *Bull's Head* by combining the saddle and handlebars of an abandoned bicycle. Congratulated on the remarkable likeness, Picasso replied, "That's not enough. It should be possible to take a bit of wood and find that it's a bird."

to be recast as monuments to Hitler. Picasso's friends, however, fearing that the fragile plasters might be damaged, secretly located a supply of bronze. Late at night they would hide his plaster models in a wheelbarrow covered with garbage, trundle them to a foundry under the very eyes of Gestapo guards, and then go through the same procedure to return the work, cast in bronze.

Among the most striking of the sculptures Picasso executed is the *Man with a Sheep*. He began to make pencil sketches of the idea in 1942. In the summer of 1943 he set to work one day with a huge mound of clay stolen for him by a Spanish friend. The finished statue, later cast in bronze, is one of the rarest works in Picasso's entire repertoire; in its style it is almost like Renaissance sculpture.

By 1944 Nazi reverses on the battlefield incited a new series of atrocities against the French, especially those of Jewish ancestry. The Gestapo uprooted Max Jacob from the monastery where he lived and threw him into a concentration camp. He died there of maltreatment only five months before France was liberated. His body was returned to Paris for burial. Picasso attended the funeral; many of his friends, fearing reprisal from the Germans, did not.

Widespread despair over such tragedies as Jacob's death was offset by the knowledge that the course of the war had turned. In June of 1944 Allied armies landed in Normandy and began a steady thrust toward Paris. As hope spread through the city, Picasso—perhaps never more French—added a new subject to his painting: views of Paris. They were almost all scenes of the Seine bridges, featuring Notre Dame, with Sacré Coeur, a landmark of his old Montmartre days, perched high on the hill overlooking the city. Most of these landscapes were painted in low key, largely blacks and grays, with a few in purples and lavenders. Then in the first week of August, brighter color came back to Picasso's palette. A tomato plant that he kept on his window sill began to bear fruit and in the four pictures that Picasso painted of it, the reddening tomatoes added a cheery note to his otherwise monochromatic canvases.

On August 24 full-scale fighting broke out in the streets, and all day Picasso's studio—like nearly every other building in Paris—shook with the sound of tanks and heavy gunfire. While others took shelter, Picasso went to work. To celebrate the imminence of Allied victory, he set before him a reproduction of *The Triumph of Pan*, the bacchanal painted by the great 17th Century French Classicist, Nicolas Poussin, and without following the forms literally, made a free copy of it.

On the following day Allied troops entered the city, and Paris went wild. Old friends, reporters and curious soldiers promptly besieged Picasso's studio; the procession kept up for days. Immediately Picasso became a new kind of hero—not just a liberated painter, as he had already been for nearly 40 years, but a symbol of tenacity throughout the bleak days of occupation. "This was not the moment for a creative man to throw in the sponge, accept defeat and stop work," he later recalled. "There was nothing to do but go on working seriously and enthusiastically struggle to find food, calmly continue to see one's friends, and await freedom." Now freedom was at hand at last.

Picasso fashioned the statue below in his Paris studio during World War II. Its peaceful, pastoral theme—it is called *Man with a Sheep*—was perhaps his reaction to the tenseness of the times. The sculpture evolved from a series of sketches, like the one above, which Picasso studied, off and on, for a year before he started working in three dimensions. Once he began modeling the clay, it took him just one day to do the figures.

A Decade
of Violence

One of history's bloodiest, bitterest civil wars burst across Spain in July 1936. Picasso watched with mounting apprehension and indignation as his native land was torn by the succession of blows that began with rebellion in Spanish Morocco and led to the savage bombing of the little town of Guernica in northern Spain the following spring. Horror-struck at the destruction of this peaceful village and its innocent civilian population by German planes and pilots borrowed from Hitler, Picasso was jolted into a whirlwind of creative fury.

As civil war in Spain gave way to the cataclysm of World War II, Picasso's paintings reflected violence, agony and death. Often he conveyed the tragedy of the time in provocative symbols such as those that fill his masterwork *Guernica (gatefold, pages 137-139)*. In other canvases, the havoc of the moment exploded in tortured renderings such as the woman weeping at the right.

When the war was over Picasso remarked, "I did not paint the war. . . . But there is no doubt that the war is there in the pictures which I painted then." Only *Guernica*, painted before the war, and *Charnel House*, completed after it, include direct references to the holocaust of war itself. But it is in the distortion of familiar subjects—screaming horses, grisly animals, broken children and tormented adults—that Picasso has made a more stunning portrait of war's cruel reality than even a camera could record.

Furiously biting a handkerchief, enormous tears streaming from the staring eyes of a ravaged face, this woman seems about to shatter under the twin impacts of grief and rage. Although the model for the painting may have been Picasso's handsome mistress Dora Maar, its inspiration no doubt was the bloody civil war in Spain.

Woman Weeping, 1937

132

Early in the 1930s, as conflict and insurrection beset Spain, Picasso began to be increasingly preoccupied with violence. Time and again in a series of brilliantly executed etchings, he explored the theme of the Minotaur—a savage mythological beast, half-man and half-bull. Sometimes Picasso stressed the human aspect of the creature, picturing its playful antics with beautiful women, but often he emphasized its ferocious other side, and the romp became rape. The series was climaxed with *Minotauromachy*—shown above. Here, a fearless little girl confronts the beast, who wears a menacing bison's head. Directly in the Minotaur's path, a defenseless woman matador with her breasts exposed slumps precariously across a disemboweled horse. The action is arrested in the electrifying second before the beast viciously tramples the fallen matador and gores the little girl.

In 1937, the implied violence of the *Minotauromachy* burst onto canvas in Picasso's most powerful painting, perhaps the greatest antiwar statement in art. Reacting to the brutal bombing of the Spanish village Guernica, he adapted the Minotaur theme in a gigantic tapestry of horror. The picture is huge—nearly 12 feet high and 26 feet across. It is cast in darkness, as if in mourning; Picasso had restricted his palette to severe blacks, dead whites, deep grays.

Near the center of the painting is a dying horse, a bloodcurdling vision of futile protest from whose contorted mouth issues an almost audible shriek of pain. To the left, a dead soldier clutches a shattered sword and nearby a mother grieves hysterically over her dead baby; to the right, a terror-struck head floats between two frantic figures that panic in the darkness. Above them all is the bull, dispassionate, perhaps triumphant—a symbol, Picasso says, of "brutality and darkness."

Lift and unfold; do not tear. ▶

It is difficult to imagine that the humble doodle shown above gave birth to *Guernica*. Yet this is what happened. Between the first of May 1937 and the end of June, when the 312-square-foot canvas was completed,

Picasso prepared 45 sketches. The two above, made the first day, already contain vital elements that would emerge in the final composition: in both the outline of the bull is at the left, the light bearer appears at the top,

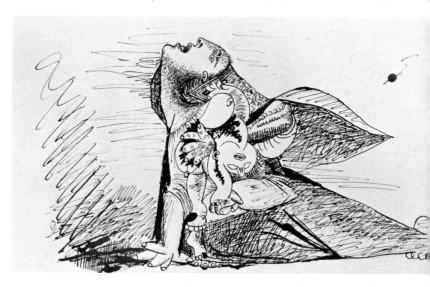

May 2, 1937

May 9, 1937

and the horse is the central figure. Tracing the evolution of these elements through four of the sketches for the whole composition *(above)*, and comparing the detail studies below with the finished painting on the gatefold, provide a unique opportunity to observe the steps in the creation of this work of genius. To do so, as Picasso once said, may enable the viewer to "discover the path followed by the brain in materializing a dream."

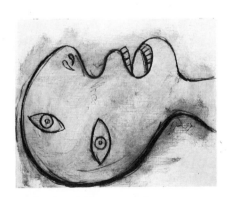

May 2, 1937

May 9, 1937

and the horse is the central figure. Tracing the evolution of these elements through four of the sketches for the whole composition *(above)*, and comparing the detail studies below with the finished painting on the gatefold,

provide a unique opportunity to observe the steps in the creation of this work of genius. To do so, as Picasso once said, may enable the viewer to "discover the path followed by the brain in materializing a dream."

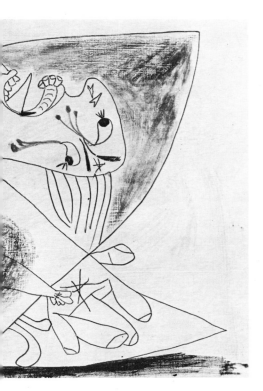

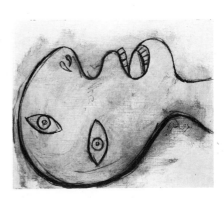

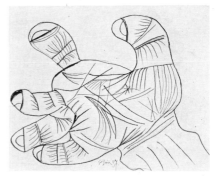

136

Guernica, 1937

Portrait of Maya with a Doll, 1938

During the last bloody year of the Spanish Civil War and the first harrowing months of World War II, Picasso's art became agonized and shrill. He transformed simple, everyday subjects, such as a cat and a bird *(left)*, into bizarre images that vividly speak of cruelty. And he took almost perverse liberties with anatomy, as the gruesome nude below illustrates. Even his pretty little daughter Maya *(above)* became sinister; her face is a grotesque fusion of both a profile and a full-face view; her smile is diabolical. The catastrophes of war, no longer pictured directly as in *Guernica*, are nonetheless present here.

Cat Devouring a Bird, 1939

Woman Dressing Her Hair, 1940

Death's Head, 1944. Side view, above; front view, right

Picasso stubbornly refused to leave Paris throughout four perilous years of Nazi occupation. He continued to work as always, his genius now focused sharply on tragedy. His interest in sculpture, dormant for nearly a decade, was roused again. *Death's Head*, a moving piece cast in bronze that his friends pilfered from the Germans, is shown here in two views to suggest its massiveness. Its ravaged surface evokes the texture of rotting flesh on a skull with vacant, staring eye sockets.

After the Allies liberated Paris in 1944, the city was shocked by news that millions of persons had been brutally slaughtered in Nazi concentration camps. Picasso's response to the carnage was a painting recalling the power of *Guernica. Charnel House*, shown below, mutely reckoned with bitter fact: the starved cadavers of a bound man, a woman and a child lie murdered only inches from a table spread with food. Once again, Picasso had fulfilled his own words: "Painting . . . is an instrument of war . . ." to be waged against "brutality and darkness."

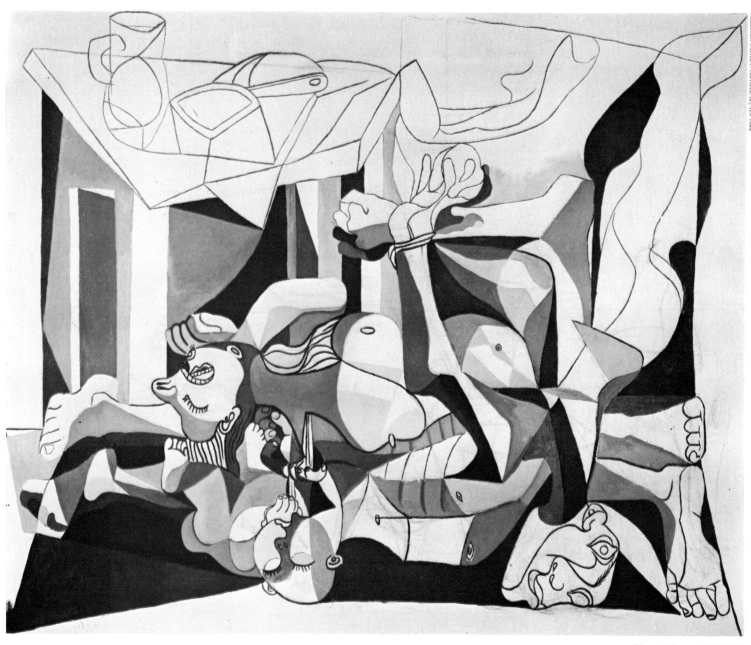

Charnel House, 1944-1945

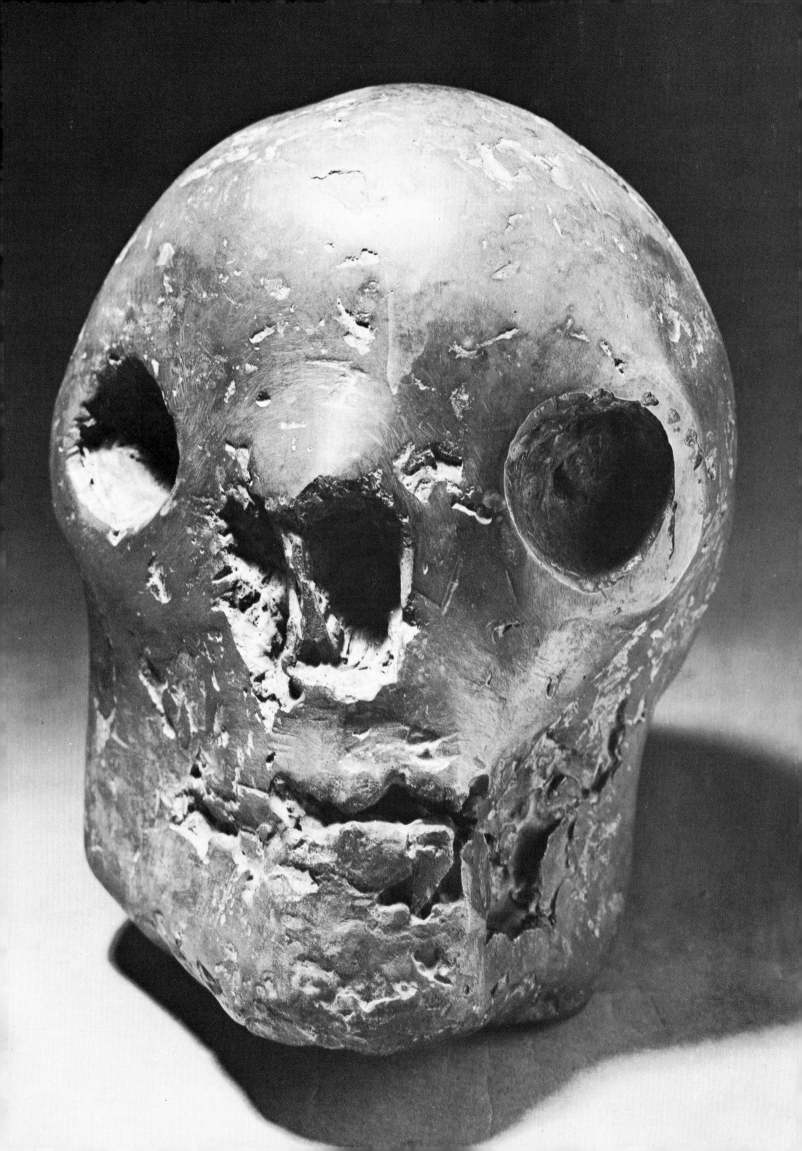

VII

The Artist
of the Century

It seemed in the fall of 1944 as if Picasso loved everybody and everybody loved him. As Paris came to life with the departure of the Germans, citizens and visiting soldiers could see him as he sat in the cafés or strolled the streets of Paris. Most Parisians agreed that he was the most popular figure of liberated France. In the view of one news correspondent, the only person who compared with him as a subject of conversation was the war hero General Charles de Gaulle.

Picasso responded to his celebrity with warmth of word and deed. He made everyone welcome at his apartment on the Rue des Grands-Augustins—old friends, journalists and total strangers. Some were soldiers who arrived so tired that they dropped off to sleep; one visitor counted 20 slumbering men in the studio on a single day. In a burst of conscience, he plunged into public service; when General de Gaulle, by now President of the Provisional Government of France, instituted a committee to choose artists to paint the war, Picasso served on it. In an even more active spirit, about a month after the liberation, he joined the French Communist Party. He gave it more than his name; he attended meetings and was soon to contribute his talent.

Most Frenchmen took Picasso's political venture with equanimity. The Communist Party in Europe was generally held in esteem at the time, for the best organized resistance against the Nazis had come from the Communists. Besides, many intellectuals saw in Communist theory a humanitarian creed and dedication to social justice. Some of Picasso's closest friends were Communists, among them Paul Éluard, who probably induced him to join, and Louis Aragon, a blue-eyed, prematurely white-haired poet. To those who took exception to his politics, charging him with caprice, Picasso retorted: "What do you think an artist is? An imbecile who has only his eyes if he is a painter, or ears if he is a musician, or a lyre at every level of his heart if he is a poet . . .? On the contrary, he is at the same time a political being. . . . No, painting is not done to decorate apartments. It is an instrument of war for attack and defense against the enemy."

Six weeks after the Liberation, the Salon d'Automne opened its doors

Picasso's piercing dark eyes retained all his life the depth and magnetism that they showed in the photograph made 58 years earlier (page 6). Although his own eyes seemed to remain unchanged over the years, his treatment of eyes in his pictures was extraordinarily diverse.

for the first time since the Germans had occupied Paris four years before. For years the Salon d'Automne had held the most important of all the exhibits in Paris in the course of any season. It had particular meaning in 1944, for it expressed the triumph of survival; it was jubilantly named the "Salon de la Libération." Giving homage to the hero of the hour, the jurors of the Salon offered Picasso a gallery to himself. The Salon had previously given this honor to outstanding French painters, but never before to a foreigner. Picasso's acceptance was as unique as the invitation itself. Unlike many artists—Matisse among them—he had made it a practice not to show his works with the paintings of other artists. But responding to the Salon gesture as he did to other demands on his new role as a public figure, he sent to the exhibition five sculptures and over 70 paintings. Most had been executed since 1940, and all were new to the public.

Emotions were taut and patriotism ran high after four years of Nazi occupation, and many people resented a foreigner's having so great an honor at such a historic moment. Two days after the exhibition opened, a mob stormed the gallery shouting: "Take them down! Money back! Explain!" They tore Picasso's pictures from the walls until officials squelched the riot; then a group of pro-Picasso students moved in to take turns guarding the gallery. Most of the rioters were young, and they were probably inspired both by reactionary artists, who had not yet accepted Picasso's revolutionary art, and by right-wing politicians, who wished to demonstrate against Picasso's Communism.

As the first flush of liberation wore off, the ugly realities of war returned. The Allies pushed ahead into Germany and in the spring of 1945 began to uncover the atrocities of the Nazi concentration camps at Buchenwald, Belsen and Dachau—horrors such as the civilized world found difficult to conceive. Picasso recorded his indignation with *Charnel House (page 142)*, one of the largest canvases he had painted since *Guernica* seven years before. As in *Guernica*, stark black, white and gray expressed the tragedy, but he abandoned the symbolism of *Guernica* and painted a pile of gruesome cadavers that make an eloquent denunciation of human brutality and madness.

With *Charnel House* Picasso's anger abated. World War II ended. Picasso's outlook brightened, and he turned from nightmare to a new and happier vision—and to a new medium. The medium was lithography, a method of printing that enables the artist to make multiple copies from what is in effect a crayon sketch. In 1945 he began to work with Fernand Mourlot, the most expert lithographer in France; his shop made the posters for practically every Paris art exhibit worthy of the name. One of his forebears had produced the famous political cartoons of Honoré Daumier almost 100 years before; another had done the posters of Toulouse-Lautrec at the turn of the century.

Picasso also found a new subject and inspiration at this time—Françoise Gilot, a young girl whom he had met about a year and a half before, at a time when the high-strung Dora Maar was growing alternately demanding and aloof. Like a good many of the women who interest Picasso, Françoise was intelligent, vivacious and good-looking;

like several of them, she was strongly independent. She was scarcely into her 20s, only a third of his age. She was also a painter of some promise, and a devotee of Picasso's work; she had been among the students who had guarded his paintings at the Salon de la Libération. The fact that she was a budding painter and he a master gave each an appeal for the other that bridged the gap in their ages. At the time that they met, Françoise had some paintings on show at a small gallery in Paris. One day the woman who ran the gallery told her excitedly that "a short man with piercing dark eyes, wearing a blue-and-white striped sailor's jersey," had come in to look over her paintings, then left without a word. It was the 61-year-old Picasso come to see the work of the 21-year-old girl he had met just twice.

Françoise's childhood had prepared the way for out-of-the-ordinary interests in any case. As the only child of a stern father who had longed for a son and given his daughter a rigorous athletic training in swimming, sailing and hunting, she had had bred into her a strong sense of competition. When she met Picasso, she recalls, "I knew that here was something larger than life, something to match myself against. [He] was a challenge I could not turn down." But there was more than challenge involved. She had lived a lonely girlhood. "Now suddenly," she wrote in retrospect, "with someone who was three times as old as I was, there was from the start an ease of understanding that made it possible to talk of anything. It seemed miraculous."

Soon Françoise began to visit Picasso's studio two or three days a week, and, like her predecessors, she quickly became his model. From the fall of 1945 into the following spring, working at Mourlot's studio, he made a series of lithographs of her. At first he portrayed her realistically, as he had done initially with Olga and Dora Maar. Then, turning to painting, he devised a new style especially for her. "You're like a growing plant," he told her, and he painted her as a flower, with a stem-like body and a face surrounded by leaves or petals. The following summer, when he went back to Antibes, where he had vacationed before the war, he took Françoise along.

They stayed in Antibes through the fall, living in a few small rooms in a friend's house that was ill-suited to painting, but that situation was remedied after a fortuitous encounter with Dor de la Souchère, the energetic and quick-witted curator of the dilapidated museum at Antibes. The museum, which contained Roman artifacts and other fragments of local history, occupied part of a palace formerly owned by the Grimaldi family—its turrets appear in the background of Picasso's *Night Fishing at Antibes*. Souchère, who was busy dressing up his faded museum, nursed hopes of acquiring that painting for his scanty collection. Hearing Picasso mutter about the inadequacy of his quarters, Souchère offered him the use of a floor of the museum as a studio.

Souchère has been well paid for his generosity. He did not get the *Night Fishing*, but Picasso left him the production of that summer—a series of about 30 paintings that are light in spirit and Mediterranean in character. One of them, *Joie de Vivre*, shows a flowerlike woman, suggestive of Françoise, dancing to the tune of a flute piped by a cen-

This happy scene shows Picasso in one of his more pixie moods on the beach at Golfe-Juan on the Riviera. Shielding Françoise Gilot from the sun, he seems to be parodying a maharani-slave relationship. Although the mood here is gay, the presence of Picasso's estranged wife, Olga, in the same town made life for Françoise quite uncomfortable. On one occasion her discomfort became physical —Olga, wearing high heels, deliberately stepped on the poor girl's hands while she was lying on the beach.

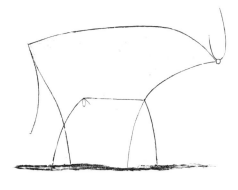

These two lithographs, both of which are simply entitled *Bull*, were done within a year of one another. At the top is the third and beneath it is the last in a series of 11 lithographs that Picasso made in 1945 and 1946. In a striking progression, he developed the figure of the animal from a meticulously realistic form to that of pure line.

taur; all are full of nymphs, fauns and centaurs, and painted in delicate pinks, blues, greens and ochers.

The episode in Antibes marked the beginning of a rush by museums to acquire Picasso's works. When he returned to Paris in the fall he had a visit from Jean Cassou, director of the Musée d'Art Moderne. Although his museum was in the heart of Paris and run by the French government, Cassou's problem was not unlike Souchère's: he had to fill out an inadequate collection. Because the major modern artists had been so much scorned during the early years of the century, no French museum ever so much as contemplated acquiring their paintings, though modern works could then have been had for a song. Now, tardy by some 30 years, the French museums woke up to the fact that their collections were woefully sparse. But Cubist art in particular was almost unobtainable. Virtually every painting was in a collector's home or in a foreign museum, many of them as a result of the sales of Kahnweiler's property in the early 1920s.

Nevertheless, Cassou hopefully went after Picasso, Braque and Léger, as well as the 77-year-old Matisse. Picasso had already determined to keep what few Cubist paintings he still owned, but he let Cassou have 10 works from recent years, among them two portraits of Dora Maar and a wartime still life. But he did not sell the paintings; he made the museum a gift of them. Not long after he had done so, the Paris newspaper *Samedi Soir* carried a story announcing that the great Picasso had rooked the tax collector. Imagine, it exclaimed, what he could write off his taxes at the end of the year!

Back on the Mediterranean coast the following summer, Picasso became the head of a family again, for Françoise had borne him a son—a black-eyed infant who strongly resembled his father. Picasso wanted to name the baby Pablo after himself, but Françoise objected on the grounds that his son by Olga was called Paulo. She remembered an 18th Century painter named Claude Gillot, and by a nice coincidence, he had painted harlequins, so they settled on Claude for the child. With his new family, Picasso more or less settled in the south of France. In 1948, a year after Claude's birth, he bought an ugly stucco house that stood on a hill near the town of Vallauris—the "Valley of Gold," as the Romans knew it, perhaps for the quality of its soil, which was excellent for making pottery.

Of late years the ancient pottery craft had declined, and Vallauris had become better known for the perfume its villagers made out of the jasmine and lavender that grew in the meadows. Still, a scattering of potters survived. On a visit to Vallauris in 1946, Picasso had met Georges and Suzanne Ramié, who managed one of the healthier workshops. Given a few lumps of clay, Picasso had fashioned three or four figurines. On returning a year later, he found to his delight that the Ramiés had fired and saved them.

Ceramics held a natural interest for Picasso, since it combined aspects of sculpture, painting and drawing; he once called it "sculpture without tears," because ceramic objects are small and easily wielded. He took it up with a passion. Just as he had done at the etching and lithographic shops of Lacourière and Mourlot, Picasso delighted in the company of the workmen, and they in turn responded warmly to his persistent questions about their craft and applauded his quick grasp of it. He had no sooner begun to learn than he surprised the experienced potters with his innovations. On one occasion, heedless of the incredulous exclamations of Mme. Ramié, he took a clay form over a yard high—it had been intended for a vase—and with swift and faultless manipulations turned it into a woman's figure, a delicate maneuver that required exquisite dexterity and sublime self-assurance. Soon he was modeling centaurs, bulls, fawns, owls and doves; and he decorated the traditional Vallauris casserole dishes and platters with scenes of bullfights, women and the animals of his painting repertory. In one year alone he produced over 2,000 pieces.

As busy as he kept himself with ceramics and painting, Picasso found time to devote to Communism. When the first of several Communist-sponsored World Peace Congresses was held in Poland in 1948, the officials asked him to attend and give an address. In the middle of August he flew with Paul Éluard to Wroclaw.

Not since the Liberation fervor had died down and the soldiers drifted out of his studio had Picasso mixed with such crowds; public sociability never came easily to him. The trip also provided his first flight in an airplane, a prospect he dreaded, and his first public address—a chore that he accomplished in a few short minutes, but one that cost him dearly in human effort. But he won no thanks from Moscow, which thoughtlessly chose that moment to issue an attack on Western art in general and him in particular. "His works," a government critic said in a Moscow magazine, "are a sickly apology for capitalist esthetics that provokes the indignation of the simple people, if not the bourgeoisie. . . . His every canvas deforms man, his body and his face." A Russian delegate rose to his feet at a dinner in Poland and echoed the charge from Moscow. Picasso paid no heed. He spent two weeks visiting Warsaw and Cracow after the festivities ended in Wroclaw.

A second Communist Peace Congress, held in Paris the following spring, caused a flurry of another kind. When the preparations for it were under way, Louis Aragon, the leading intellectual of the French Communist Party, asked Picasso to supply a poster to advertise the event. Picasso agreed, then procrastinated until one day Aragon turned up at his studio to remind him of his promise. The artist had nothing prepared, but fortunately for Aragon, Picasso had on hand a sheaf of recent lithographs, among which they found one portraying a pigeon; the bird had been a present from Henri Matisse not long before. It was not exactly a dove, but it was an exquisite drawing and a perfect specimen of lithography (Mourlot had pronounced it the finest ever made), and Aragon decided on sight it was just what he wanted. He took it away about midday, and by five o'clock that afternoon the buildings of Paris were coated with reproductions of Picasso's pigeon announcing the Communist Peace Congress.

The press set up a ruckus, and anyone in France who might have forgotten Picasso's political affiliation was reminded of it now. Cartoon-

This fanciful poster by Picasso advertises a fair at which the most popular products—flowers, perfumes, ceramics—of Vallauris, the town he had adopted, were to be displayed. "Poteries" (ceramics) were of the greatest interest to Picasso. He produced an enormous number of ceramic pieces, many of which he permitted local craftsmen to copy and sell to tourists. In the 10 years he spent there, he helped Vallauris to prosper.

CONGRÈS MONDIAL
DES PARTISANS
DE LA PAIX

SALLE PLEYEL
20·21·22 ET 23 AVRIL 1949
PARIS

ists lampooned the bird in varying ways, as a feathered Soviet tank and a Trojan horse, and a newspaper crowed that "The Cocos [French slang for Communists] have taken up the coo-coo language of the Kremlin." Picasso himself had a living reminder of the event. While the congress was in session, Françoise gave birth to a daughter, and they named her Paloma, the Spanish for "dove."

Picasso always delighted in his children, and Claude and Paloma were no exception. He played with them both constantly, as he had done before with Paulo and Maya, fashioning dolls and animals out of bits of wood and cardboard, which he decorated with crayon. He also drew and painted them and their mother. And as he had once combined Dora Maar's slender face with that of the Afghan hound Kazbek, now he merged the chubby faces of Claude and Paloma with that of the current pet, a Boxer puppy.

From all appearances, this was a period of peace in Picasso's life. Happy with the town of Vallauris, in which he was now spending much of the year, he offered the village a bronze cast of his *Man with a Sheep*, which he said he would like to have installed in the main square, where children could climb on it. The town councilors, for all they esteemed their distinguished citizen, were not so sure a Picasso would do for prominent display. What kind of sculpture was it, they wanted to know? Assured that it was just what its name implied, they agreed to accept it. Only the village blacksmith seems to have had a taste for sophisticated art. He moaned: "What a pity, if it looks like any other statue!"

Picasso was making more sculptures now. About 1950 he resumed a technique that had occupied him now and then in the past, notably in the early 1930s, when he had put together scraps of wire and pots and pans to make near-abstract constructions. But now the results were far from abstract. Probably the most famous of the later works is a goat made of a wicker basket, a palm frond and two cast-off milk pitchers that Picasso scavenged in the potters' dumping field. Attesting Picasso's magic touch, the combination is unmistakably a goat.

He also continued to serve the Communist Party—which, ironically, had in store another slap in his face. When Stalin died in 1953, Louis Aragon asked Picasso for a portrait of the dictator to use together with the obituary in *Les Lettres Françaises*, the Communist weekly he edited. Picasso had some misgivings about the project—he had never seen Stalin and had only a newspaper photograph to go by—but out of regard for Aragon, he agreed to try it. According to Françoise, the resulting portrait, a simple and generally realistic line drawing, looked exactly like her father, whom Picasso had never seen either. They laughed, she wrote, "until Pablo began to hiccough." Nevertheless, they sent it off to Aragon, who published it at once.

The Communists were not amused. The portrait did not meet their idealization of their great hero. As Picasso was too valuable an asset to trifle with, however, they directed their wrath at the hapless Aragon and ordered him to print an apology in his newspaper. As soon as news of an intraparty spat leaked out, reporters appeared on Picasso's doorstep asking if it were true "that in doing the portrait of Stalin you wanted to make fun of him?" Whether or not the party members liked the portrait was their affair, said Picasso; but "when you send a funeral wreath, the family customarily doesn't criticize your choice of flowers." Not long afterward, a joke went the rounds of Paris to the effect that Jean Cocteau had asked Picasso why he had ever joined the party in the first place. "I thought it would be a big, brotherly family," Picasso replied. "*Eh bien*, now I hate my family!"

If they could laugh over the Stalin portrait, Françoise and Picasso had many a moment that was not marked by jollity. Ever since they had begun living together, Françoise had been discovering new sides to Picasso's nature, and more and more complications to his life. She soon found that he made regular Thursday and Sunday visits to Maya and Marie-Thérèse—a practice he had kept up for years. He constantly sang their praises, together with those of Dora Maar. Olga sometimes followed Françoise and Picasso on the street or at the beach and when she was not in their vicinity, she wrote frequent letters, which Picasso read aloud to Françoise or left lying around for her perusal. She came to feel, she wrote in her memoirs, "that he had a kind of Bluebeard complex"—and indeed, he eventually began to stay away from home for days at a time, then return to boast of escapades with new women.

"For the first time," she wrote, "I started taking into account the factor of Pablo's age. Until then, it had never seemed important. But when he began gamboling about so wildly, I suddenly came face to face with the fact that he was now over 70 years old. For the first time I saw him as an old man." At the end of the summer of 1953 she left him in Vallauris and took the children to Paris.

Whatever their disagreements may have been, Françoise's departure struck Picasso a hard blow. Deserted and miserable, he turned to his work—and to a theme that had haunted him over the years, that of the artist and his model. The result was published as *Picasso and the Human Comedy*, a series of 180 drawings that constitute a hymn of praise to women and make bitter comments on age and impotence. A third of them depict an artist who often appears leering and old painting a woman who is cruelly young.

Picasso was never alone for long. Soon he was seeing more and more of a dark-eyed young woman who would stay at his side till the end. She was Jacqueline Roque, a cousin of Mme. Ramié, the potter. Jacqueline had come to visit in the fall of 1952 and had stayed on as a sales clerk at the pottery. As she shuns publicity, little is known about her. But friends said that she was better able than any of his former women to adapt to his caprices and moods. When she met Picasso, she knew a little Spanish; she set herself to learning it better and became fluent in his native language. She also spoke English, and was therefore able to serve as an interpreter between him and foreign visitors. With her native flexibility, she calmed him down in stormy moods, buoyed him up when he was low. She was always on hand but never in the way; she read quietly while he worked, and from time to time changed her outfit or her hairdo the better to serve as his model.

As on former occasions, Picasso was inspired by the new liaison to

Picasso often adapted his old Cubist technique of collage to sculpture by combining actual objects he found around him with forms that he created himself. The most striking feature of *Baboon and Young (above)* is its head, which is composed of his child's toy motor car. Surprisingly, this combination of a ready-made object and a sculptured figure—both later cast in bronze—is remarkably convincing. Most people fail to notice the toy car at first, but see, instead, a total image of mother and child.

Both paintings shown above are entitled *Venus and Cupid*. The top one was done in the 16th Century by the German master Lucas Cranach, the lower one by Picasso in 1957. Picasso often based his own work on old masterpieces, sometimes quite irreverently. Here, he has made Venus' hat into a huge sombrero, dwarfing her tiny head.

seek a change of scene. He once observed wistfully to a friend: "You know where you live, you live in Paris, you've got a house, you know where you stand. But I'm not anywhere, I don't know where I live. You can't imagine how appalling it is." Whatever the force that propelled him, he moved from place to place throughout his life—especially whenever the circumstances of his life changed. In the spring of 1955 he purchased a villa in the environs of Cannes, about five miles from Vallauris. The house, called La Californie, was a turn-of-the-century mansion, ornately decorated with Art Nouveau stone carvings and wrought-iron grillwork. A great many of the pictures that Picasso painted here were portraits of Jacqueline, clearly showing her big eyes and her high cheekbones.

Here he also undertook a major work, a set of variations on *Las Meninas* by his great 17th Century countryman Velázquez. Variations on the works of his predecessors were an old preoccupation. On the face of it, that seems rather odd for a man whose hallmark was innovation, but studying the work of others is one way by which Picasso constantly reexamined the problems of art. During the siege of Paris he had worked on a Poussin, and in the years that followed on works by Cranach, Courbet, El Greco, Manet, Giorgione and Delacroix.

Velázquez' painting *(page 160)* deals in another way with the relationship between the painter and his model. In the case of the Velázquez there is the added element of a relationship with the viewer as well. The Spanish princess and her ladies-in-waiting, who give the painting its title, seem to be the main feature of the picture as the viewer confronts it. But closer examination discloses Velázquez at his easel, facing the King and Queen, whom the viewer sees reflected in a mirror. From that it follows that Velázquez is painting the King and Queen, not their daughter and her maids; that in the painted mirror the viewer is seeing a reflection of a reflection; that the princess and her maids, who had seemed on first glance to be the major subject, are in fact only incidental; and finally, that the viewer, according to the perspective rendered by Velázquez, stands at a point from that painter that is precisely equivalent with that of the King and Queen. By such a process of logic, the viewer may actually fancy himself a subject of Velázquez' canvas.

Picasso spent two months working with Velázquez' painting. By fall he had produced 44 variations on it. Retaining his predecessor's general arrangement, he sometimes painted the figures separately, sometimes in groups. But Velázquez had achieved the illusion of the vast room by representing distance as it was done in his time, by the use of chiaroscuro and ever-diminishing objects. Picasso achieved as great an effect of distance by the Cubist technique of overlapping planes, some of them lit and others shaded, and all of them making a pattern of forms that seem to recede from the picture plane.

Picasso's series is at once a witty parody of Velázquez' masterpiece and a sober exploration of the ambiguities of art. It is also a summing up of the pictorial representations of form and space that Picasso himself had brought to modern art. In its varied treatment of light and distance and the relationship of figures to one another, the full series may be said to constitute a distillation of Picasso's life work.

In March of 1961, in his 80th year, Picasso married Jacqueline Roque, in a small civil ceremony attended only by two friends. Again he marked his change of circumstances with a change of residence. This time he moved to Mougins, where he bought a villa, named Notre-Dame-de-Vie after a 17th Century chapel that stands on a hill above it. Screened from the public by lush trees, it afforded him privacy.

He continued to be a public figure, however. In the fall of 1966 the art community of the entire Western world celebrated his 85th birthday with tributes of every description—magazine and newspaper articles, a television spectacular and exhibitions all over the world. The most lavish of these was a giant retrospective show of three months' duration in Paris, where more than 1,000 paintings, sculptures and graphics, shipped from all over the world, filled the Grand Palais, the Petit Palais and the Bibliothèque Nationale. Thousands of Frenchmen and tourists stood on long lines, waiting for a look at the largest assemblage ever seen of the works of a single painter.

Perhaps no tribute to Picasso is more touching than that given him by his countrymen in Spain, where two of his works, the *Dream and Lie of Franco* and *Guernica*, long ago made him *persona non grata* with the dictatorship. Since 1963 Barcelona has boasted a Picasso Museum that holds 500 sculptures, graphics, drawings and paintings—many given by proud countrymen. Some came from unknowns, and at least one is a gift of Surrealist Salvador Dali. The museum itself is largely due to the efforts of Jaime Sabartés, who devoted to the project three years of his time and 427 pieces given him by Picasso since their boyhood. Together with the mayor of Barcelona, Sabartés persuaded the city officials to donate a 15th Century Gothic palace in the Calle de Montcada, a street in the district where Picasso lived as a youth. The artist himself donated a number of his works, and more were promised from collectors. When the museum opened its doors in 1963, in the face of the official silence of the Spanish government, the Spanish press covered the event with fanfare, and the museum is well visited both by Spaniards and by tourists.

Until his death Picasso continued to create paintings, sculptures, engravings, etchings, lithographs—and with stunning diversity. He no longer spoke in full voice as he once did to practicing artists. He ceased to innovate or surprise and he no longer was the leader of the vanguard. But in an era marked by repeated innovations, he was in the forefront for half a century. And the legacy of his long lifetime of prolific work continues to enrich and inspire other artists. Hardly a painter has lived since the First World War who has not taken Picasso's work into account; not a student of art has omitted it from his curriculum; scarcely a museum of modern art anywhere in the Western world lacks an example of his production.

Perhaps the best summation of his genius has been given by his good friend Gertrude Stein. More than 30 years ago she wrote: "He alone among painters did not set himself the problem of expressing truths which all the world can see, but the truth which only he can see."

In August 1967, a 50-foot-high steel sculpture by Picasso was erected at the new Civic Center in Chicago. The piece had been donated by the artist to the city, which he had never visited, but which he greeted with "My warmest friendship." So huge that it had to be constructed by the American Bridge Company, the sculpture was based on Picasso's 42-inch-high model *(above)*, which he later gave to The Art Institute of Chicago. Picasso, in his customary refusal to explain his work, never identified it. Greeted by both praise and derision, the sculpture may represent the head of a woman.

The Enduring Themes

Picasso's later works have none of the revolutionary character of his earlier periods. He was not involved in new art movements that arose in his later years —Abstract Expressionism, Op and Pop Art. Rather, he continued to explore the world around him in decorative paintings that bear the stamp of his maturity in the sureness and inventiveness of their line, in the broad freedom of their color, and in the enduring quality of their themes. Again and again he returned to subjects drawn from his personal life—women, mothers and children, his home and, above all, art itself. In pictures like the one at right, a variation on an old master, he attempted to come to grips with the history of art, and tried, it seems, to find his special place in it.

His vigor was undiminished; after World War II an almost constant stream of sculpture, drawings, lithographs and even an entirely new form for him —ceramics—came from his hand. His productivity, which consisted principally of paintings and sculpture, was phenomenal: one critic has estimated that during the course of his lengthy career Picasso created some 50,000 works of astonishing variety.

Picasso once said that "to search means nothing in painting. To find is the thing." On the following pages are some of the things he "found," along with a selection of his own statements, made at various times during his career, about art.

In this imaginative reworking of a portrait by El Greco, the 16th Century Spanish master who was a strong influence on Picasso for many years, much of the original remains clearly intact, but Picasso has translated it into his own distinctive stylistic language.

Portrait of a Painter after El Greco, 1950

154

155

First Steps, 1943

The theme of maternity is a strong and lasting one in Picasso's work. He treated it in several media and several styles, as the two works shown here suggest. While the war was still raging in Europe, Picasso painted the hopeful scene at the far left, of a child learning to walk with his mother's help. The women's sad eyes and the jagged outlines of the child's body convey the grim atmosphere of the times, but a sense of optimism is clear.

When, at the age of 67, Picasso himself became a father again, he made the amusing sculpture below. It is created from scrap materials —Cocteau once called Picasso "King of the Ragpickers"—a broken-down baby carriage, pot shards, a gas ring from a stove, all miraculously united into a charming and convincing image.

When asked about his habit of precipitously switching from one form of expression to another, sculpture to painting, for example, Picasso had said, "Pictures are never finished in the sense that they suddenly become ready to be signed and framed. They usually come to a halt when the time is ripe, because something happens which breaks the continuity of their development. When this happens it is often a good plan to return to sculpture."

Woman with a Baby Carriage, 1950
COLLECTION PICASSO

157

Undoubtedly the greatest sources of inspiration throughout Picasso's long career were the women who shared his life. After the war there were two: Françoise Gilot, and Jacqueline Roque, whom he married in 1961. The statue of a pregnant woman at right was inspired by Françoise. She recalls that Picasso wished her to have a third child, but that she did not want to. So, expressing his wish in the way that he knew best, Picasso made the sculpture—the very quintessence of pregnancy. As with many of his late sculptures, he started this one with "found" objects—three water jugs that he picked up from a trash pile form the basis for the figure's rounded breasts and swollen belly. But when the piece was cast in bronze, the objects had been so carefully modeled into the form that they were no longer recognizable.

The painting of Jacqueline on the opposite page is one of many, in a wide variety of styles, in which Picasso has explored her fine features; a long, straight nose, large eyes and an elegant neck. He has portrayed her in naturalistic drawings and wildly colorful, almost abstract paintings, each somehow capturing a sense of the woman. Picasso was loath to talk about technique, but one of his rare statements on the subject applies peculiarly well to this portrait: "When you draw a head, you must draw like that head. . . . Ingres drew like Ingres, not like the things he drew. If, for instance, you take a tree. At the foot of the tree there is a goat, and beside the goat a little girl tending the goat. Well, you need a different drawing for each. The goat is round, the little girl is square, and the tree is a tree. And yet people draw all three in the same way. That is what is false. Each should be drawn in a completely different way."

Pregnant Woman, 1950

Portrait of J.R. with Roses, 1954

Diego Velázquez: *Las Meninas*, 1656

Picasso painted many variations on old masters, among which are 44 versions of a Velázquez court scene *(above)*. At the right, he has transformed Velázquez' mastiff into a dachshund, his family pet. Elsewhere he showed the boy in the foreground playing a piano while hanging like a marionette.

"I saw the little boy with a piano. The piano came into my head and I had to put it somewhere. For me he was hanged so I made him hang. Such images come to me and I put them in. They are part of the reality of the subject. Reality is more than the thing itself. I always look for its superreality. Reality lies in how you see things. A green parrot is also a green salad *and* a green parrot. He who makes it only a parrot diminishes its reality. A painter who copies a tree blinds himself to the real tree. I see things otherwise. A palm tree can become a horse. Don Quixote can come into *Las Meninas*."

Las Meninas, October 3, 1957

Las Meninas, August 17, 1957

Picasso's environment always provided him with a source of art. When he was 19, he immortalized his cramped Paris atelier in *The Blue Room (pages 26-27)*, and over the years he regularly painted the places in which he lived and worked. Some are obviously recognizable; some are not. "Nature and art are two different things," Picasso once declared. "In art we express our conception of what is not visible in nature."

Shown here are two "interior landscapes," as Picasso called them, that were painted of his Riviera house *La Californie*, where Picasso provided a dovecote *(right)* for his beloved and familiar pets. In the picture below, the flower petal-like windows of *La Californie* serve as a decorative backdrop for the artist's cluttered studio room. At the center, commanding the viewer's attention, is a blank canvas. It is a perfect symbol of an unending, and often excruciating, challenge: "The most awful thing for a painter is the white canvas."

The Studio at Cannes, 1956

The Pigeons, September 11, 1957

Art itself was one of Picasso's most frequent subjects. And nowhere did he express himself better than in a series of paintings, "The Artist and His Model," one of which is shown here. In this version, the painter, wearing a hat and ornate boots, is seated before a heavy easel, his dog at his side; he is in and of the world. The model, on the other hand, is diaphanous; like a vision she becomes a part of the background, perhaps expressing Picasso's notion of the elusiveness of art, the painter's real subject.

Yet Picasso's art is never wholly abstract; he always gives clues to his subject. "You know, it's like being a peddler. You want two breasts? Well, here you are—two breasts. What is necessary is that the fellow who looks at the canvas should have at hand everything he may need: you must be sure it's all there for him. Then he'll put everything in place with his own eyes."

Making "sure it's all there" was an unending problem for Picasso, as it is for all artists. "Worst of all is that [the painter] never finishes. There's never a moment when you can say 'I've worked well and tomorrow is Sunday.' As soon as you stop, it's because you've started again. You can put a picture aside and say you won't touch it. But you can never write 'The End.' "

164

The Artist and His Model, April 2-6, 1963

165

A Portrait of the Artist

Picasso was the most successful artist of the 20th Century. Museum directors, commercial art dealers and wealthy connoisseurs vied for possession of his creations, and prices for his major works have soared into the hundreds of thousands of dollars. His Blue Period painting, *Mother and Child at the Seashore,* for example, was sold in 1967 for a staggering $532,000—at that time the highest price ever paid for the work of a living artist. This astonishing popularity has led to a more thorough documentation of Picasso's life and art than that of any other artist in history. Scholars, critics, journalists, an Army private, two ex-mistresses, and a world-famous psychoanalyst have dissected every aspect of his many styles, shifting moods, daily habits, and even his love affairs, in hundreds of books and thousands of articles, written in every major language.

The portrait of Picasso created by this deluge of words has been given an additional dimension with the aid of photojournalism. Noted photographers like Arnold Newman, who made the portrait at left in Picasso's villa at Cannes on the French Riviera, were permitted on occasion to breach Picasso's self-imposed isolation. Another famed photographer, David Douglas Duncan, was even more fortunate, for he spent better than three months with Picasso off and on during the mid-1950s. During this time, Duncan shot more than 10,000 photographs. This huge collection—sampled on the following pages —shows Picasso at work and with his family, his friends and his pets in an intimate and detailed portrait of art's most celebrated figure.

Although Picasso sometimes allowed himself to be photographed in his leisure moments he often refused to permit professional photographers to shoot pictures of him at work; usually only intimate friends and members of his family were granted that privilege. But after a time, the artist accepted Duncan's constant but unobtrusive presence during the creative process. In the sequence below Picasso completes a painting called *The Beach at*

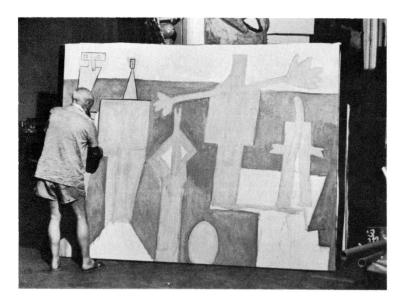

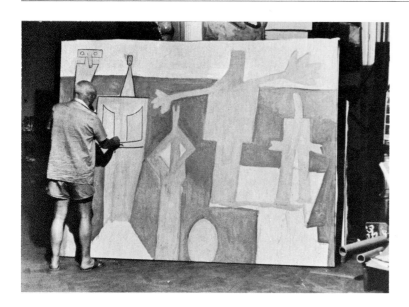

Garoupe, showing a snorkel-nosed skindiver *(far left)*
and four other swimmers.

Unlike adults, who must remain silent in the studio
while the artist works, youngsters are special and can do as
they please. But when Picasso's children came to visit
from Paris, where they lived with their mother, Françoise
Gilot, the artist put aside his work and romped in his
studio with Paloma, eight, and Claude, ten *(overleaf)*.

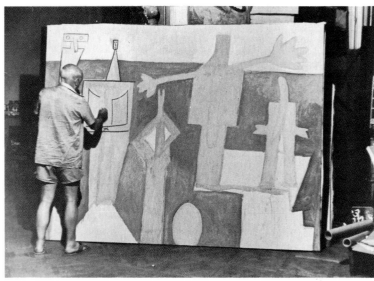

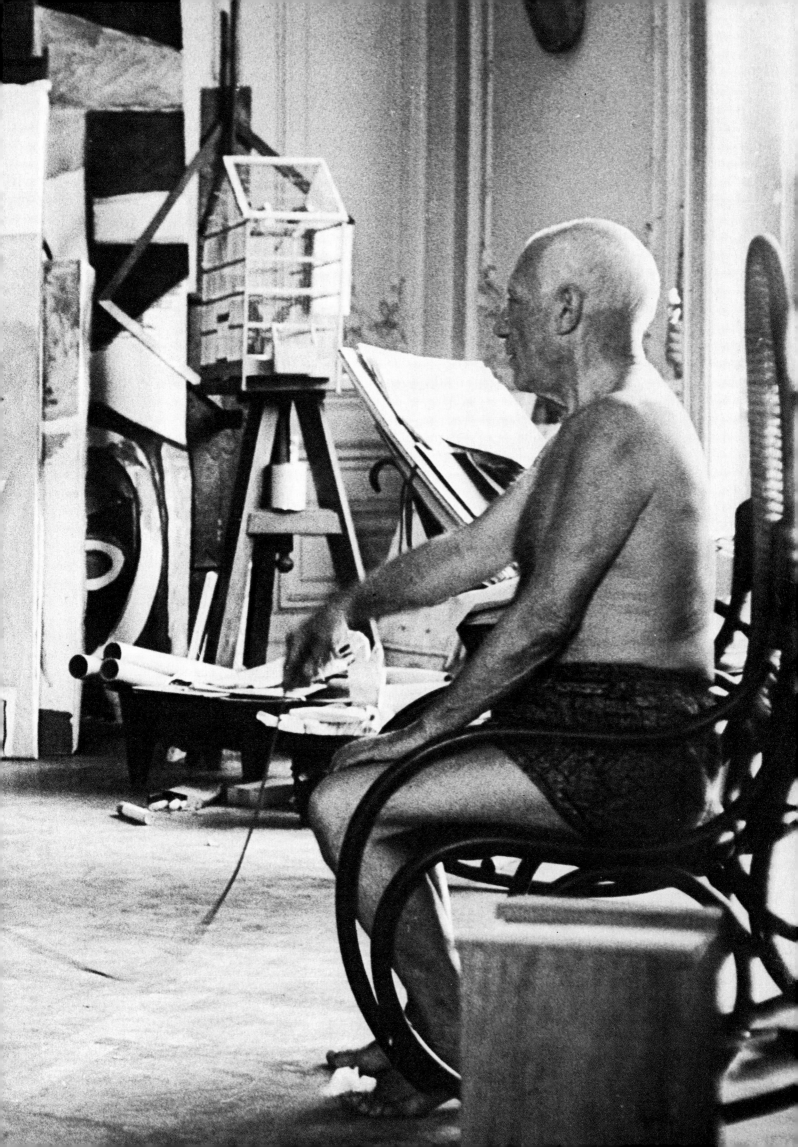

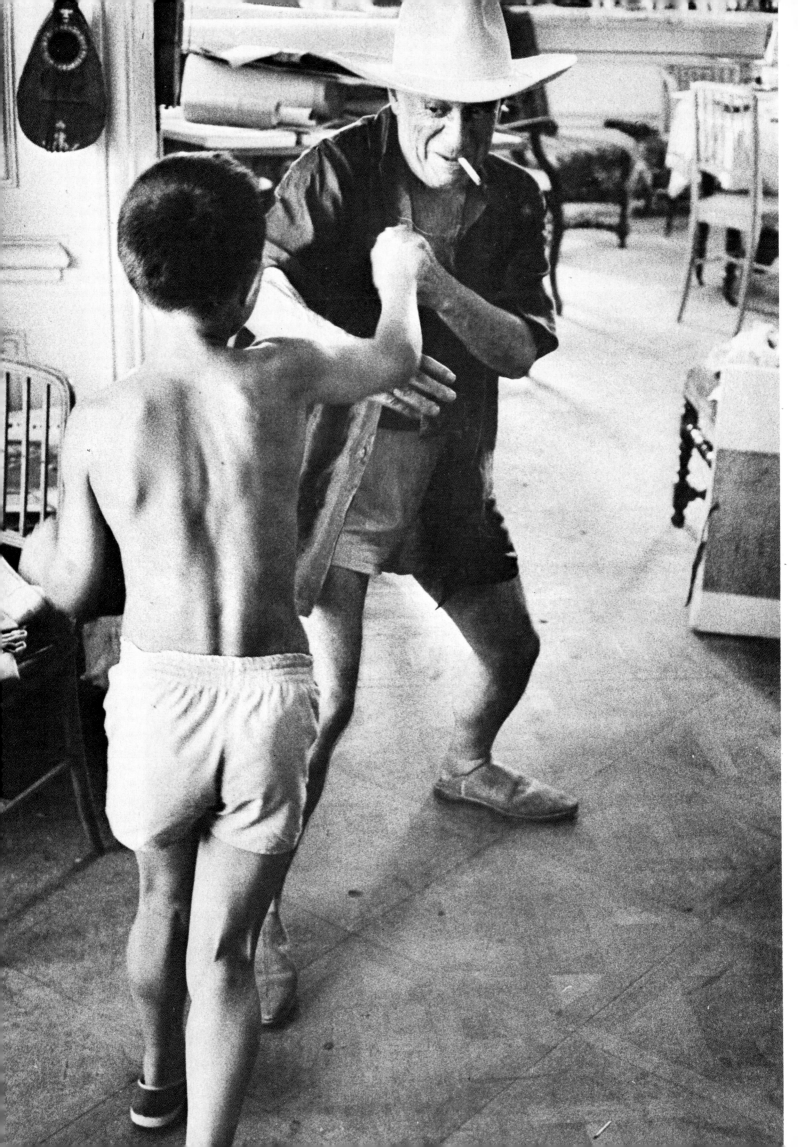

Picasso's home was a child's paradise. Scattered through its rooms and jamming every available surface were such intriguing items as bizarre masks, bugles, guitars, ladders, oversize hats, wooden crates the size of playhouses, and boxes of tantalizing bric-a-brac. To Picasso every object was always a possible subject for a composition, but to children they possessed the exciting lure of an inexhaustibly stocked toyshop.

In the pictures shown here, Picasso, like a typical father, became an incurable ham actor when Claude and Paloma arrived for a visit. Making use of various "props," at one moment he donned a cowboy hat and squared off with Claude; another time Picasso's famous pet goat stole the show as Jacqueline, the artist's wife *(center, below)*, entertained Paloma *(left)* and her friends.

Quieter temptations lay about his studio—sheets of blank paper, colored pencils and brimming paste pots—and while the master cut a linoleum block for a poster for a forthcoming exhibition, Paloma *(right)* found a box of crayons and became absorbed in her own work.

Picasso's artistic wizardry enabled him to utilize the most commonplace subjects or transform others to make pieces for which collectors have paid dearly. Over the years he fashioned a guitar from bits of string, nails and a newspaper; a mother baboon's head out of a toy car; and a charming assemblage from a pin, a few matches and a butterfly.

One of these magical feats occurred as Picasso was lunching on *sole à la meunière*—fish in butter sauce. As he methodically stripped the skeleton of its last morsels (*opposite*), an idea struck him. Suddenly he jumped from the table and dashed to his studio. A few moments later he returned with a slab of moist potter's clay.

As shown in the two-row sequence of photographs above, he first lifted the skeleton from his plate and pressed it into the clay to form fossil-like imprints. Next, using a knife, he trimmed the excess clay from his "fillets" and then daubed a large unfired platter with paint. Two of the clay fossils were then pressed directly onto the plate, and, finally, the piece was prepared for firing.

Something was missing, for, as photographer Duncan observed, Picasso's ceramic looked drab. The artist reassured him: "Don't worry, Dooncan, those colors will all change in the fire up at the kiln. This will be emerald. That will be blue. But won't these fish be surprised when they discover they've lost their bodies somewhere."

175

Screech Owl, 1949

Red-and-White Owl, 1953

Masquerade—Owl with the Head of a Man, 1953

Ceramics had become part of Picasso's repertoire during the 1940s, when he visited, for the second time, the kilns at Vallauris. The pottery of this unprepossessing village in southern France had been known ever since the days of the ancient Romans. Jugs, pots, plates and compotes made from the fine, abundant clay had flowed from the wheels of local artisans.

Picasso's pottery took almost as many shapes as his sculpture. At times he made household utensils like the plates and jugs shown below. While these objects

Bullfight and Spectators, 1952

Two Fish, 1957

Head of a Bull, 1957

176

Lady with a Mantilla, 1949

Seated Woman, 1953

Woman in a Long Gown, with Loose Hair, 1953

retain their basic utility, their surfaces, decorated with bulls, fish and other favorite subjects, bring to mind his canvases. At other times he fashioned such charming pieces as the owls *(above, left)*, which have no other function than that of decoration.

Perhaps Picasso's most fascinating creations in this medium are those that were launched as one thing but were transformed into something else by Picasso's nimble imagination. The three pieces *(above, right)*, for example, were vases before they were women. Picasso turned their handles into human arms, reshaped their basic forms to make breasts, waists and hips, then painted in faces and dresses. Finally he added a brilliant finish—in some pieces unique combinations of colors and glazes—and sent them off to the kilns of Vallauris to be fired. For Picasso, creating such pieces was a delightful exercise in whimsy. But his immensely popular contributions have widely revived interest in ceramics as an art form and more specifically brought new prosperity to the potters of Vallauris.

Medley of Bulls, 1958

Double Visage, 1952

Large Bird, 1961

177

From the dawn of his career, bullfighting was among Picasso's favorite subjects. Time and again he returned to that spectacle in some of his most brilliant creations. The most comprehensive treatment of the theme was made in the 1950s, when he produced 35 etchings to illustrate a classic text on bullfighting.

First, he painted each composition on a mirror-smooth sheet of copper *(above)*. Then, after he etched the images into his plates with acid, each scene was printed. The three prints at right, which show the emotion-charged opening procession, a pirouetting *banderillero*, and an unlucky matador being gored, are stunning evidence of the economy and precision of Picasso's brushwork, for each figure is barely more than a stroke, a dot or a flourish.

Advancing age and the time-consuming demands that accompany fame conspired against Picasso's gregariousness. After World War II, he settled into the seclusion of his home and his visitors were limited to friends. The writer Jean Cocteau (who died in 1963) was one of the most frequent of Picasso's callers, and on one occasion the two took turns hammering out a lusty tune on an African marimba *(opposite)*.

Picasso also enjoyed the company of movie stars, and the late Gary Cooper was one of his favorites. Cooper *(right)* once presented the artist with a Colt .45 revolver, and the two men passed the afternoon gleefully blasting away at a tin can. Neither could hit it. When French actors Simone Signoret and Yves Montand *(at left, below)* paid a visit, on the occasion pictured here, a heated argument about Communism erupted, but Picasso chose not to take sides. When social interludes such as these came to an end, Picasso reclaimed his solitude, at times to work, at others to ponder completed works or to dream of those still to be born *(overleaf)*.

Chronology: Artists of Picasso's Era

	1825	1875	1925	1975

SPAIN
- JULIO GONZALEZ 1876-1942
- PABLO PICASSO 1881-1973
- JUAN GRIS 1887-1927
- JOAN MIRÓ 1893-
- SALVADOR DALI 1904-
- OSCAR DOMINGUEZ 1906-1958
- ANTONIO TAPIÈS 1923-

ITALY
- UMBERTO BOCCIONI 1882-1916
- GINO SEVERINI 1883-1966
- AMEDEO MODIGLIANI 1884-1920
- GIORGIO DE CHIRICO 1888-1978
- GIORGIO MORANDI 1890-1964

SWITZERLAND
- THÉOPHILE STEINLEN 1859-1923
- PAUL KLEE 1879-1940
- ALBERTO GIACOMETTI 1901-1966
- JEAN TINGUELY 1925-

GERMANY
- LOVIS CORINTH 1858-1925
- EMIL NOLDE 1867-1956
- LYONEL FEININGER 1871-1956
- FRANZ MARC 1880-1916
- ERNST LUDWIG KIRCHNER 1880-1938
- MAX BECKMANN 1884-1950
- MAX ERNST 1891-1976
- HANS HARTUNG 1904-
- WOLFGANG SCHULZE WOLS 1913-1951

HOLLAND
- VINCENT VAN GOGH 1853-1890
- PIET MONDRIAN 1872-1944
- BRAM VAN VELDE 1895-

BELGIUM
- JAMES ENSOR 1860-1949
- PAUL DELVAUX 1897-
- RENÉ MAGRITTE 1898-1967

ENGLAND
- BEN NICHOLSON 1894-
- HENRY MOORE 1898-
- GRAHAM SUTHERLAND 1903-
- VICTOR PASMORE 1908-
- FRANCIS BACON 1910-
- ALAN DAVIE 1920-

FRANCE
- PIERRE PUVIS DE CHAVANNES 1824-1898
- GUSTAVE MOREAU 1826-1898
- JEAN-PAUL LAURENS 1838-1921
- PAUL CÉZANNE 1839-1906
- AUGUSTE RODIN 1840-1917
- CLAUDE MONET 1840-1926
- HENRI ROUSSEAU 1844-1910
- PAUL GAUGUIN 1848-1903
- GEORGES SEURAT 1859-1891
- ARISTIDE MAILLOL 1861-1944
- PAUL SIGNAC 1863-1935
- HENRI TOULOUSE-LAUTREC 1864-1901
- PIERRE BONNARD 1867-1947
- EDOUARD VUILLARD 1868-1940
- HENRI MATISSE 1869-1954
- GEORGES ROUAULT 1871-1958
- JACQUES VILLON 1875-1963
- RAYMOND DUCHAMP-VILLON 1876-1918
- MAURICE VLAMINCK 1876-1958
- KEES VAN DONGEN 1877-1968
- FRANCIS PICABIA 1879-1953
- ANDRÉ DERAIN 1880-1954
- ALBERT GLEIZES 1881-1953
- FERNAND LÉGER 1881-1955
- GEORGES BRAQUE 1882-1963
- LOUIS MARCOUSSIS 1883-1941
- JEAN METZINGER 1883-1956
- ROBERT DELAUNAY 1885-1911
- ROGER DE LA FRESNAYE 1885-1925
- LE CORBUSIER (CHARLES EDOUARD JEANNERET) 1887-1965
- JEAN ARP 1887-1966
- MARCEL DUCHAMP 1887-1968
- JACQUES LIPCHITZ 1891-1973
- ANDRÉ MASSON 1896-1965
- YVES TANGUY 1900-1955
- JEAN DUBUFFET 1901-
- JEAN BAZAINE 1904-
- EDOUARD PIGNON 1905-
- BALTHUS (BALTHASAR KLOSSOWSKY) 1908-
- FRANÇOIS GRÜBER 1912-1948
- NICOLAS DE STAËL 1914-1955
- PIERRE SOULAGES 1919-
- GEORGES MATHIEU 1921-

	1825	1875	1925	1975

Picasso's predecessors and contemporaries are grouped chronologically according to country. The bands correspond to the life-spans of the artists.

Bibliography   *Paperback

PICASSO'S LIFE

Blunt, Anthony, and Phoebe Pool, *Picasso: the Formative Years*. Viking Press, Inc., 1962.
Brassaï, *Picasso & Co.* Doubleday & Company, Inc., 1966.
Duncan, David Douglas, *The Private World of Pablo Picasso*.* Ridge Press, 1958.
Elgar, Frank, *Picasso*. Frederick A. Praeger, Inc., 1955.
Gilot, Françoise, and Carlton Lake, *Life with Picasso*.* Signet Books, 1964.
Olivier, Fernande, *Picasso and His Friends*. Appleton-Century, 1965.
Palau I Fabre, Josep, *Picasso en Cataluña*. Ediciones Polígrafa, S.A., Barcelona, 1966.
Penrose, Roland:
    Picasso: His Life and Work.* Schocken Books, Inc., 1962.
    Portrait of Picasso.* Museum of Modern Art, 1957.
Sabartés, Jaime:
    Picasso: documents iconographiques. Pierre Cailler, Geneva, 1954.
    Picasso: An Intimate Portrait. Prentice-Hall, Inc., 1948.
Stein, Gertrude, *Picasso*.* Beacon Press, 1959.
Uhde, Wilhelm, *Picasso and the French Tradition*. Weyhe, 1929.
Vallentin, Antonina, *Picasso*. Doubleday & Company, Inc., 1963.

PICASSO'S ART

Arnheim, Rudolf, *Picasso's Guernica*. Faber & Faber, Ltd., London, 1962.
Barr, Alfred H., Jr., *Picasso: Fifty Years of His Art*. Museum of Modern Art, 1946.
Buchheim, Lothar-Günther, *Picasso*. Thames and Hudson, London, 1959.
Daix, Pierre, *Picasso*.* Frederick A. Praeger, Inc., 1965.
Daix, Pierre, and Georges Boudaille, *Picasso 1900-1906*. Éditions Ides et Calendes, Neuchâtel, 1966.
Duncan, David Douglas, ed., *Picasso's Picassos*. Harper & Row, Publishers, 1964.
Elgar, Frank, *Picasso: Cubist Period*. Tudor Publishing Company, 1956.
Éluard, Paul, *Picasso*. Philosophical Library, Inc., 1947.
Geiser, Bernhard, ed., *Picasso: 55 Years of His Graphic Work*. Harry N. Abrams, Inc., 1962.
Horodisch, Abraham, *Picasso as a Book Artist*. World Publishing Co., 1962.
Jaffé, Hans L. C., *Picasso*. Harry N. Abrams, Inc., 1964.
Janis, Harriet and Sidney, *Picasso: The Recent Years: 1939-1946*. Doubleday & Company, Inc., 1946.
Kahnweiler, Daniel-Henry, *The Sculptures of Picasso*. Rodney Philips & Co., London, 1949.
Parmelin, Hélène:
    Picasso: The Artist and His Model. Harry N. Abrams, Inc., 1965.
    Picasso: Intimate Secrets of a Studio at Notre-Dame-de-Vie. Harry N. Abrams, Inc., 1967.
    Picasso: Women. Éditions Cercle d'Art, S.A., Paris, and Harry N. Abrams, N.V., Amsterdam, 1967.
Quinn, Edward, *Picasso at Work*. Doubleday & Company, Inc., 1965.
Ramié, Georges, *Picasso: Pottery*.* Tudor Publishing Company, 1962.
Sabartés, Jaime, and Wilhelm Boeck, *Picasso*. Harry N. Abrams, Inc., 1955.
Zervos, Christian, *Pablo Picasso*. 17 vols. Cahiers d'Art, Paris, 1932-1966.

ARTISTS AND WRITERS OF THE TIMES

Apollinaire, Guillaume:
    Calligrammes. Gallimard, Paris, 1925.
    The Cubist Painters. George Wittenborn, Inc., 1962.
Barr, Alfred H., Jr., *Matisse: His Art and His Public*. Museum of Modern Art, 1951.
Brinnin, John Malcolm, *The Third Rose*. Little, Brown & Co., 1959.
Crespelle, Jean-Paul, *The Fauves*. New York Graphic Society, 1962.
Davies, Margaret, *Apollinaire*. Oliver and Boyd, 1964.
Duthuit, Georges, *The Fauvist Painters*. George Wittenborn, Inc., 1950.
Flanner, Janet, *Men and Monuments*. Harper & Row, Publishers, 1964.
Perruchot, Henri, *Cézanne*. Grosset and Dunlap, Inc., 1963.
Russell, John, *Braque*. Phaidon Art Books, 1959.
Salmon, André, *Souvenirs Sans Fin*. Gallimard, Paris, 1955.
Shattuck, Roger, *The Banquet Years*.* Doubleday & Company, Inc., 1961.
Sprigge, Elizabeth, *Gertrude Stein: Her Life and Work*. Harper & Row, Publishers, 1957.
Steegmuller, Francis, *Apollinaire: Poet among the Painters*.* Farrar, Straus and Company, 1963.
Stein, Leo, *Journey into the Self*. Crown Publishers, Inc., 1950.
Toklas, Alice B., *What Is Remembered*. Holt, Rinehart and Winston, Inc., 1963.
Vallier, Dora, *Rousseau*. Harry N. Abrams, Inc., 1962.
Van Vechten, Carl, *Selected Writings of Gertrude Stein*. Random House, Inc., 1946.
Vollard, Ambroise, *Recollections of a Picture Dealer*. Little, Brown & Co., 1936.

Bibliography (continued)

CATALOGUES

Hommage à Pablo Picasso. Ministère d'État, Affaires Culturelles, Ville de Paris, 1966.
Picasso. The Arts Council of Great Britain, 1960.
Picasso. Philadelphia Museum of Art, 1958.
Picasso: 75th Anniversary Exhibition. Museum of Modern Art, 1957.
Picasso: 60 Years of Graphic Works. Los Angeles County Museum of Art, 1967.
Richardson, John, ed., *Picasso: An American Tribute.* Produced in cooperation with Chanticleer Press, 1962.
Years of Ferment. UCLA Art Council, 1965.

ART HISTORICAL BACKGROUND

Fry, Edward F., *Cubism.* McGraw-Hill Book Company, 1966.
Golding, John, *Cubism: History and an Analysis 1907-1914.* George Wittenborn, Inc., 1959.
Habasque, Guy, *Cubism.* Albert Skira, Geneva, 1959.

Kahnweiler, Daniel-Henry, *The Rise of Cubism.* George Wittenborn, Inc., 1949.
Rewald, John:
    History of Impressionism. Museum of Modern Art, 1961.
    Post-Impressionism from Van Gogh to Gauguin. Museum of Modern Art, 1962.
Rosenblum, Robert, *Cubism in the Twentieth Century.* Harry N. Abrams, Inc., 1960.
Schmutzler, Robert, *Art Nouveau.* Harry N. Abrams, Inc., 1964.
Selz, Peter, and Mildred Constantine, eds., *Art Nouveau.* Museum of Modern Art and Doubleday & Company, Inc., 1959.
Sypher, Wylie, *Rococo to Cubism in Art and Literature.** Vintage Books, 1960.

MISCELLANY

Courthion, Pierre:
    Montmartre. Albert Skira, Geneva, 1957.
    Paris in Our Time: From Impressionism to the Present Day. Albert Skira, Geneva, 1957.
Herbert, Eugenia W., *The Artist and Social Reform.* Yale University Press, 1961.
Thomas, Hugh, *The Spanish Civil War.* Harper & Row, Publishers, 1961.
Vlaminck, Maurice, *Dangerous Corner.* Abelard-Schuman, Ltd., 1961.

Acknowledgments

For their help in the production of this book the author and editors wish to thank the following people: Juan Ainaud de Lasarte, Director, Museo Picasso, Barcelona; Luis Alegro Nuñez, Director, Escuela de Bellas Artes, Real Academia de San Fernando, Madrid; Madame Odette Arnaud; René and Claire Batigne; Heinz Berggruen; J. D. Bernal; Mrs. Demaree Bess; Sir Anthony Blunt; Brassaï; Palma Bucarelli, Superintendent, Galleria Nazionale d'Arte Modèrna, Rome; John Carter; A. Cirici-Pellicer; Salvador Dali; David Douglas Duncan; Juan Gaspar Paronella, Director, Sala Gaspar, Barcelona; Maurice Jardot, Director, Galerie Louise Leiris, Paris; Daniel-Henry Kahnweiler; Louise Leiris; Federico Marès Deuloval, Director, Escuela de Bellas Artes y Oficios de Barcelona; Stavros Niarchos; Josep Palau I Fabre; Drue Tartiere Parsons; Natalie Perrone; Jaime Sabartés; Eleanore Saidenberg; Pierre Schneider; José Selva Vives, Assistant Curator, Museos Municipales de Barcelona; Timothy Simon; Germaine Tureau, Chief, Section Commerciale de la Photothèque des Musées Nationaux, Paris; Jean and Nicole Valdeyron; Marie-Thérèse Walter.

Picture Credits

The sources for the illustrations in this book appear below. Credits for pictures from left to right are separated by semicolons, from top to bottom by dashes. When no credit for a picture is given the original source is unknown or the owner wishes to remain anonymous.

All the works of Pablo Picasso which appear in this book and the work by Auguste Renoir on page 21 are published by arrangement with SPADEM, by French Reproduction Rights, Inc. The works on pages 56, 72, 93, 95, 97, 98-99, appear by arrangement with ADAGP, by French Reproduction Rights, Inc.

SLIPCASE: Pierre Boulat

CHAPTER 1: 6—Ediciones Polígrafa, S. A., Barcelona. 8,9—Pierre Cailler. 10,11—David Douglas Duncan. 12—La Photothèque. 13—From *Pablo Picasso* by Christian Zervos, Cahiers d'Art, Paris 1954, Vol. 6, plate 47. 14,15—Foto Más except third from top right O'Hana Gallery, London. 17—David Douglas Duncan. 18—Augusto Meneses. 19—Upper left Apolinar Gallardo—courtesy André Held. 20—From *Picasso en Cataluña*, Ediciones Polígrafa, S. A., Barcelona. 21—Giraudon—Giraudon—Scala. 22,23—Augusto Meneses; Yves Debraine. 24—National Gallery of Art; The Metropolitan Museum of Art—National Gallery of Art. 25—The Metropolitan Museum of Art. 26,27—Henry B. Beville.
CHAPTER 2: 28—David Douglas Duncan. 30—The Museum of Modern Art—André Martin. 32—Bottom Kohlhammer-Bildarchiv, Stuttgart. 33—Augusto Meneses. 35—Bottom H. Roger Viollet. 36—The Baltimore Museum of Art—The Museum of Modern Art. 37—Joe McKeown for TIME. 38—Gertrude Stein Collection, Yale University Library. 39—The Baltimore Museum of Art. 41—Yves Debraine. 42,43—Pierre Boulat. 44—The Art Institute of Chicago. 45—The Solomon R. Guggenheim Museum. 46—The Art Institute of Chicago. 47—Scala. 48,49—National Gallery of Art; Dmitri Kessel. 50—Scala—John Schiff. 51—Lee Boltin.
CHAPTER 3: 52—A. J. Wyatt. 55—From *Henri Rousseau* by Dora Vallier, Harry N. Abrams, Inc., New York, 1964, plate 69. 56—Galerie Louise Leiris, Paris. 57—From *Pablo Picasso* by Christian Zervos, Cahiers d'Art, Paris, 1942 Vol. 2, part 2, plate 372. 58—Galerie Maeght, Paris. 65—Robert S. Crandall. 66—The Metropolitan Museum of Art. 67—Giraudon; A. J. Wyatt; David Douglas Duncan—The Museum of Modern Art; courtesy Éditions d'Art Albert Skira; David Douglas Duncan. 68—The Museum of Modern Art. 69—Augusto Meneses; Don Getsug from Rapho Guillumette; Pierre Boulat—Photothèque Musée de l'Homme; Robert S. Crandall; Pierre Boulat. 70,71—A. J. Wyatt—Pierre Boulat; The Museum of Modern Art.
CHAPTER 4: 72—The Art Institute of Chicago. 74—La Photothèque. 76—From *Pablo Picasso* by Christian Zervos, Cahiers d'Art, Paris, 1942, Vol. 2, plate 405—Cliché Musées Nationaux. 77—The Museum of Modern Art. 79—The Museum of Modern Art—La Photothèque. 80—Bottom from *Pablo Picasso* by Christian Zervos, Cahiers d'Art, Paris, 1954, Vol. 6, plate 1429. 82, 83—The Museum of Modern Art. 84—Dmitri Kessel. 85—Galerie Beyeler, Basel—Dmitri Kessel. 87—Eric Schaal. 88—National Gallery of Scotland; Heinz Zinram. 89—Karl Roodman. 90—Dmitri Kessel—Pierre Boulat; Pierre Boulat. 91—The Art Institute of Chicago. 92—The Solomon R. Guggenheim Museum. 93—The Museum of Modern Art. 94,95—Pierre Boulat; Philadelphia Museum of Art—A. J. Wyatt. 96—Pierre Boulat. 97—Cliché Musées Nationaux. 98,99—Albright-Knox Art Gallery. 100,101—A. J. Wyatt; Lee Boltin.
CHAPTER 5: 102—Hence Griffith. 104—Courtesy Marie-Thérèse Walter. 105—Grunwald Graphic Arts Foundation, University of California by Ivor Protheroe. 106—Brassaï. 107—Eric Schaal—from *Picasso, An Intimate Portrait*, by Jaime Sabartés, Prentice-Hall, Inc., New York, 1948—also from *Picasso, An Intimate Portrait*—Museo Picasso, Barcelona. 108—The Museum of Modern Art. 109—Lee Miller. 113,114—Pierre Boulat. 115—Lee Boltin—Fogg Art Museum. 116,117—Scala; David Douglas Duncan. 118-120—David Douglas Duncan. 121—The Museum of Modern Art—Robert S. Crandall; David Douglas Duncan; Pierre Boulat. 122—Scala. 123—The Museum of Modern Art.
CHAPTER 6: 124—Pierre Boulat. 126—The Museum of Modern Art. 127—Top from *Jane's All the World's Aircraft*, 1938 Volume. 128—Lee Miller. 129—La Photothèque. 130—Galerie Louise Leiris, Paris. 131—La Photothèque—Dmitri Kessel. 133—Derek Bayes. 134-136—The Museum of Modern Art. 137-139—The Museum of Modern Art by Soichi Sunami. 140,141—Pierre Boulat; David Douglas Duncan—Frank Lerner. 142—Brassaï—Galerie Louise Leiris, Paris. 143—Photo Chevojon.
CHAPTER 7: 144—Arnold Newman. 147—Robert Capa from Magnum. 148—From *Picasso, 55 Years of His Graphic Art*, Harry N. Abrams, Inc., New York and Amsterdam, 1965, plate 122—The Museum of Modern Art. 149—The Museum of Modern Art. 150—From *Art in Posters* by Fernand Mourlot, George Braziller, New York, 1959. 151—The Museum of Modern Art. 152—Scala—Pierre Boulat. 153—The Art Institute of Chicago. 155,156—Pierre Boulat. 157,158—Dmitri Kessel. 159—David Douglas Duncan. 160,161—David Douglas Duncan except top left Lee Boltin. 162,163—David Douglas Duncan. 164,165—Pierre Boulat. 166—Arnold Newman. 168-175—David Douglas Duncan. 176—Eddy Van Der Veen except center—Yves Debraine courtesy Mr. and Mrs. S. and G. Ramié; courtesy Galerie Louise Leiris, Paris; Yves Debraine. 177—Eddy Van Der Veen; Henri Mardyks; Henri Mardyks—Yves Debraine; Henri Mardyks; Eddy Van Der Veen. 178,179—David Douglas Duncan; Cosmopress, Geneva, courtesy Verlag Gerd Hatje. 180-183—David Douglas Duncan.

Index

Numerals in italics indicate a picture of the subject mentioned. Unless otherwise identified, all listed art works are by Picasso. Dimensions are given in inches except where indicated; height precedes width.

The text for this book was photocomposed in Bodoni Book, a typeface named for its Italian designer, Giambattista Bodoni (1740-1813). One of the earliest modern typefaces, Bodoni Book differs from more evenly weighted old-style characters in the greater contrast between thick and thin parts of letters. The Bodoni character is vertical with a thin, straight serif.

PRINTED IN U.S.A.